Learn Every Day About Colors

Edited by Kathy Charner

Learn Every Day About COLORS

BEST IDEAS from TEACHERS

EDITED BY
Kathy Charner

© 2009 Gryphon House, Inc.
Published by Gryphon House, Inc.
P.O. Box 207, Beltsville, MD 20704
800.638.0928; 301.595.9500; 301.595.0051 (fax)

Visit us on the web at www.gryphonhouse.com

Illustrations: Deb Johnson
Cover Art: Stock photos

Library of Congress Cataloging-in-Publication Information:
Learn every day about colors / edited by Kathy Charner.
    p. cm.
 ISBN 978-0-87659-088-1
1. Colors--Study and teaching (Preschool)--Activity programs. 2.
Education, Preschool--Activity programs. I. Charner, Kathy.
 QC496.L43 2009
 535.6--dc22

                              2008044698

BULK PURCHASE

Gryphon House books are available for special premiums and sales promotions as well as for fund-raising use. Special editions or book excerpts also can be created to specification. For details, contact the Director of Marketing at Gryphon House.

DISCLAIMER

Gryphon House, Inc. and the authors cannot be held responsible for damage, mishap, or injury incurred during the use of or because of activities in this book. Appropriate and reasonable caution and adult supervision of children involved in activities and corresponding to the age and capability of each child involved is recommended at all times. Do not leave children unattended at any time. Observe safety and caution at all times.

Table of Contents

INTRODUCTION 7

ART ACTIVITIES

3+
Class Color Mural...........................9
Green Fun....................................10
Junk Flowers 11
My Favorite Color Collage 12
Rain Painting................................13
Same-on-Same Painting 14
Stained-Glass Doors 15

4+
Blue, Blue Sky 16
Color Blending..............................17
Let's Cut Some Colors! 18

BLOCK ACTIVITY

3+
Building with Color 19

BOOK ACTIVITIES

3+
Harold & the Purple Crayon...........20
Mary Wore Her Red Dress 21
What Makes the Color Green? 22

4+
Caps for Sale................................23
Colorful Honey 24
Kitten Coloring.............................25
My Crayons Talk...........................26

CIRCLE OR GROUP TIME ACTIVITIES

3+
Color Pops 27
Circle Color Game 28
Color Circle 29
Color Search 30
Color Watch 31
Hurry Up! Pick One Up! 32
Leaves Are Falling..........................33
Swatch Match 34
What Color Are You?......................35
Who Do You See?..........................36

4+
Color Band Connections 37
My Cat's Favorite Color..................38

DRAMATIC PLAY ACTIVITIES

3+
Color Picnic 39
Dressing the Mascot......................40
Shoe Store 41

GAME ACTIVITIES

3+
Butterfly Bonanza..........................42
Color Basket 43
Color Card Game...........................44
Colorful Caterpillars 45
Find Your Favorite Color 46
I Can Sing a Rainbow 47
It's a Match 48
Rainbow Soup 49
Sock Walk.....................................50

4+
Color Game 51
Make It Whisper! A Marker Game..52
Secondary Color Match-Up............53

5+
Carton o' Primary Colors 54
Color Bingo...................................55
What's My Color? 56

LANGUAGE AND LITERACY ACTIVITIES

3+
Colorful Handprints 57
I Spy Colors in a Bottle 58

4+
Matching Color Word Cards...........59

MATH ACTIVITIES

3+
Button Count 60
Cereal Mania 61
Color Cans....................................62

Colorful Ribbon Cups.....................63
Fishing for Colors 64
My Favorite Melon.......................65
What Color Will Your Doll Wear?...66

5+
Following Directions 67
Graph Us 68

MORNING GREETING ACTIVITY

3+
Good Morning, Color 69

MUSIC AND MOVEMENT ACTIVITIES

3+
Color Hokey Pokey 70
Color Song....................................71
Colorful Xylophone 72
Moving Colors...............................73
Musical Colors 74
T-Shirt Dance...............................75

4+
Rhythmic Gymnastics....................76

OUTDOOR PLAY ACTIVITIES

3+
Color Dash 77
Fly Away, Colors!...........................78
Rainbow Run 79
Spot That Shirt! 80

4+
Traffic Lights..................................81

SCIENCE AND NATURE ACTIVITIES

3+
Color Walk....................................82
Food for Thought 83
Hand Mixing.................................84
A Rainbow of Water Colors 85

4+
Be a Chameleon 86
Color-Coordinated Cuisines 87
Eye Color (Graph) 88
Ladybugs Are Black and Red 89
What Is Blue?................................90

5+
Flowers Are Many Colors 91

SMALL MOTOR ACTIVITIES

3+
Sorting Buttons..............................92

5+
Not-So-Hungry Caterpillar 93

SNACK AND COOKING ACTIVITIES

3+
Colorful Snack: An End-of-Topic
  Celebration 94
Cream Cheese Colors....................95
Green Fruit Salad 96

4+
Fruit Rainbow 97

5+
Make a Shake 98
Yummy Colors...............................99

SONGS, POEMS, AND FINGERPLAY ACTIVITIES

3+
Color, Color, Disappear!...............100
Color-Match March.....................101
Suzy Had a Bright Red Dress.......102
Where Is Blue Bird? 103

4+
Cats Come in Many Colors...........104
Color Patterns Song.....................105
Five Little Crayons.......................106

TRANSITION ACTIVITIES

3+
Color Me Gone............................107

4+
Color Captain 108

INDEXES

Index of Children's Books.............109
Index 115

Note: The books listed in the Related Children's Books section of each activity may occasionally include books that are only available used or through your local library.

Introduction

You have in your hands a great teacher resource! This book, which is part of the *Learn Every Day* series, contains 100 activities you can use with children ages 3–6 to help them develop a lifelong love of learning, as well as the knowledge and skills all children need to become successful students in kindergarten and beyond. The activities in this book are written by teachers and professionals from the field of early childhood education—educators and professionals who use these activities in their classrooms every day.

The activities in this book are separated by curriculum areas, such as Art, Dramatic Play, Outdoor Play, Transitions, and so on. The activities are organized according to their age appropriateness, therefore activities for children age three and older come first, then activities for children age four and older, and finally, activities for children five and older. Each activity has the following components— learning objectives, a list of related vocabulary words, a list of thematically related books, a list of the materials (if any) you need to complete the activity, directions for preparation and the activity itself. Also included as part of each activity is an assessment component to help you observe how well the children are meeting the learning objectives. Given the emphasis on accountability in early childhood education, these assessment strategies are essential.

Many activities also contain teacher-to-teacher tips that provide smart and useful ideas, including how to expand the central idea of an activity in a new way or where to find the materials necessary to complete a given activity. Some activities also include related fingerplays, poems, or songs that you can sing and chant with the children. Children love singing, dancing, and chanting. These actions help expand the children's understanding of an activity's learning objectives.

This book, and the other books in this series, give early childhood educators 100 great activities that require few materials, little if any preparation, and are sure to make learning fun and engaging for children.

Class Color Mural

3+

LEARNING OBJECTIVES

The children will:
1. Work with a variety of materials and art media in a given color.
2. Develop their small motor skills.

Materials

marker
poster board
long white paper
small red collage items
  (feathers, leaves,
  colored tape, glitter,
  sequins, torn paper,
  stickers, ribbon,
  yarn, elastic bands,
  pompoms)
red art materials
  (crayons, colored
  pencils, markers,
  pastels, paints)

VOCABULARY

black	green	purple	yellow
blue	gray	red	
brown	orange	silver	
gold	pink	white	

PREPARATION

● Attach long white paper to the wall or floor. Place various small materials in appropriate containers.

WHAT TO DO

1. Tell the children, "We are making a red picture today! What are things that are red?"
2. Write their ideas on a piece of poster board and then show the children the selection of red materials you have gathered.

3. Let them work together to create a red mural on the paper and then display the work in the classroom or school. Before taking it down, review what the children have learned by asking them to identify the materials they contributed.

ASSESSMENT

To assess the children's learning, consider the following:
● Can the children individually discuss their contributions to the mural, as well as those of their classmates?
● Can the children successfully attach different materials to the mural?

Children's Books

How Is a Crayon Made?
  by Oz Charles
*Polar Bear, Polar Bear,
What Do You Hear?* by
  Bill Martin, Jr.

Patrick Mitchell, Yagoto, Nagoya, Japan

Green Fun

3+

LEARNING OBJECTIVES

The children will:

1. Identify and name the primary colors.
2. Recognize what happens when one primary color is mixed together with another primary color.

VOCABULARY

hue   primary color   secondary color   tint

PREPARATION

- Write each child's name with a permanent marker on a resealable bag.
- Provide blue and yellow fingerpaint and a plastic spoon.

WHAT TO DO

1. Read *Little Blue and Little Yellow* by Leo Lionni.
2. Invite the children to retell the story using blue and yellow felt circles and a flannel board.
3. Have each child open up his bag and put one spoonful of both blue and yellow fingerpaint into it. Zip the bags closed and help the children tape the tops of their bags using strong clear tape, such as library tape.
4. The children will enjoy gently "squishing" the two colored paints together and watching what happens to the blue and yellow paint.
5. When they are finished mixing the paint, ask the children if they would like to paint with their new color (green). Provide fingerpaint paper for them to paint with the new color they created!

ASSESSMENT

To assess the children's learning, consider the following:

- Can the children identify colors? (Record their answers.)
- Can the children explain what happens when you mix two primary colors together?
- Can the children predict the secondary color that will come from mixing two primary colors?
- Can the children follow verbal directions?

Kaethe Lewandowski, Centreville, VA

Materials

Little Blue and Little Yellow by Leo Lionni
blue and yellow felt circles
flannel board
blue and yellow fingerpaint
plastic spoon
sandwich-size resealable bags
strong, clear tape
fingerpaint paper

Children's Books

Color Dance by Ann Jonas
Colors/Los Colores by Clare Beaton
Red, Blue, Yellow Shoe by Tana Hoban
White Rabbit's Color Book by Alan Baker

Junk Flowers

3+

LEARNING OBJECTIVES

The children will:

1. See and learn to recognize different colors.
2. See and learn to recognize color words (blue or red, for example).
3. Sort and use different colors and materials.

Materials

thick paper or card stock
paints
variety of materials in each color you want to study
bits of colored/silver paper
scissors (adult only)
tape
glue
pens
index cards

VOCABULARY

color names
collage
combination

descriptive words for materials (shiny, soft)

flower

PREPARATION

- Collect a variety of scrap materials. Choose a different type of material for each color you want to study. The children will be making a wall display of collage flowers, each from a different color and from a different type of material (for example, bits of yellow fabric for a yellow flower or red cellophane candy wrappers for a red flower).
- Cut the materials into small pieces.

WHAT TO DO

1. Ask the children to paint a background for the flowers on thick paper. Let dry.
2. Encourage the children to draw interesting original flower shapes on paper or card stock. Cut out the shapes.
3. Have the children paint or color with pens (in the chosen color) the shapes you cut out.
4. Invite the children to glue the colored materials to each flower shape.
5. When the flowers are dry, have the children tape them onto the big display.
6. Write the color names used on the board. Ask the children to copy the color names onto the index cards and add them to the display.

ASSESSMENT

To assess the children's learning, consider the following:

- Can the children sort materials and make decisions about why to use certain colors of certain materials?
- Can the children recognize colors and label them with the correct names?

Jane Moran, Stockport, England, United Kingdom

Children's Books

Elmer's Colors by David McKee
The Rainbow Fish by Marcus Pfister
What Color Is Your Underwear? by Sam Lloyd

My Favorite Color Collage 3+

LEARNING OBJECTIVES

The children will:

1. Create a collage using shades and tints of a single color of their choosing.
2. Utilize small motor skills to glue materials on the collage.
3. Recognize and classify colors.

Materials

paper in various colors
magazine clippings
paint in various colors
glue sticks
pompoms in various
    colors
collage materials

VOCABULARY

collage	favorite	shade	tint
darker	lighter		

PREPARATION

● Arrange materials on a table for the children to choose from.

WHAT TO DO

1. Ask the children what their favorite color is.
2. Show the children the materials and tell them they can make a collage using their favorite color.
3. Explain to the children that they can choose only one color to use in their collage, but they can use darker and lighter shades of that color. Talk about different shades and tints of colors.
4. While they are working, ask the children questions about their collages.
5. Have the children help clean up and wash their hands (if necessary).

TEACHER-TO-TEACHER TIP

● Ask the children guided questions as they work to help them extend their learning and to check their understanding: "Tell me about your collage." "Why is _____ your favorite color?" "Other than on your collage, where are places you see your favorite color?"

ASSESSMENT

To assess the children's learning, consider the following:

● Are the children able to select and use materials that are in various shades and tints of their favorite color?
● Are the children displaying an age-appropriate level of small motor function while working with the materials?

Children's Books

Cat's Colors by
Jane Cabrera
*Chidi Only Likes Blue:
An African Book
of Colors* by
Ifeoma Onyefulu

Angela Rathbun, Centennial, CO

Rain Painting

LEARNING OBJECTIVES

The children will:

1. Identify colors when they are mixed in different ways.
2. Imagine what might happen to paint when rain or water hits it.
3. Learn to create a hypothesis on what will happen to the paint colors.
4. Accept that what one predicts is not what always happens.

Materials

painting paper
electrical or strong
    tape
paint
paintbrushes
writing paper and
    pencils
rain or watering can
    and water

VOCABULARY

combination	mix	predict	soak
hypothesis/	moisten	prism	
hypotheses			

PREPARATION

● Put out paper with paint and brushes.

WHAT TO DO

1. Try this activity on a rainy day. If it is not a rainy day, substitute a watering can filled with water.
2. Each child will paint a picture using any colors he chooses.
3. Before putting the children's paintings outside in the rain, ask each child to dictate to you or write down what he thinks will happen to the colors on his painting. Will the children be happy with the outcome? What colors will mix well and what colors will not?
4. Using strong electrical or duct tape, tape the paintings on the pavement outside and see what happens to them when the rain (or water from the watering can) hits them. Were their hypotheses correct?

ASSESSMENT

To assess the children's learning, consider the following:

● After reading each child's hypothesis on what he thinks will happen when his painting gets wet, ask the children questions about what they think will happen to their paintings and why. Listen to the children talk to each other about their paintings.
● Are the children able to identify the colors?

Annette Rivlin-Gutman, Seattle, WA

Children's Books

Mouse Paint by Ellen Stoll Walsh
Red with Other Colors by Victoria Parker
White with Other Colors by Victoria Parker
Yellow with Other Colors by Victoria Parker

Same-on-Same Painting

3+

LEARNING OBJECTIVES

The children will:

1. Explore with various shades of colors.
2. Create a picture using a monochromatic painting technique.
3. Learn about dark and light shades of a color.

Materials

paper and paint of the
  same (or similar)
  color
paintbrushes
white and black paint
spoons and paper cups
paint shirts

VOCABULARY

artist	color	shades (light,	technique
base	monochromatic	lighter, dark,	
	original	darker)	

PREPARATION

- For younger children, premix paint shades, one with a few drops of white and one with a drop or two of black.

WHAT TO DO

1. Provide cups of various colors of paint, as well as cups (or bowls) of white paint and black paint. Provide spoons for the children to use to scoop drops of the shade paints (black and white) into the colored paint.
2. Help the children create containers of lighter and darker shades of paint by adding white and black paint to each paint color. Older children can mix their own shades. When mixing the paint, keep in mind that a little bit of black goes a long way. Older children may want to chart the numbers of drops they mix in to make different shades of colors.
3. Ask the children to talk about the paint colors, and then ask what happens as they add white and black paint. Use the words *light, lighter, dark,* and *darker.*
4. Hang the pictures on a drying rack or clothesline to dry. Be sure to place a cloth or paper under the area to catch paint drips.
5. Consider playing classical music or quiet instrumental music while the children paint.

Children's Books

Looking at Paintings: An Introduction to Fine Art for Young People by Erika Langmuir
Warthogs Paint: A Messy Color Book by Pamela Duncan Edwards

ASSESSMENT

To assess the children's learning, consider the following:

- Talk with the children about the concept of a monochromatic painting. Can they name the original colors of their paintings?
- Can the children describe how they made new shades of colors for their paintings?

Sandra Nagel, White Lake, MI

Stained-Glass Doors

LEARNING OBJECTIVES

The children will:
1. Learn to recognize colors.
2. Develop their small motor skills by gluing shapes to paper.

Materials

9" x 12" black
    construction paper
construction paper in
    assorted colors
scissors (adult only)
glue
pictures of stained-
    glass windows from
    cathedrals

VOCABULARY

Gothic arch   lead   shape names   stained glass
                                   (circle, square,
                                   triangle,
                                   rectangle)

PREPARATION

- Fold 9" x 12" black construction paper in half vertically and trim the top third edge to resemble a Gothic (pointed) arch, similar to a stained glass window in a cathedral.
- Cut 1" construction paper squares, triangles, and rectangles in assorted colors.

WHAT TO DO

1. Show the children the pictures of stained glass windows. Tell them that when the workers made the windows, they put lead between the small pieces of glass to make the picture.
2. Give each child a piece of black paper cut to resemble a Gothic window.
3. Encourage the children to glue the small shapes to the black paper. Explain that they can make their own pictures look like the ones you showed them if they leave a space between the shapes when they glue them on.

ASSESSMENT

To assess the children's learning,
    consider the following:
- Ask the children to describe the images they have made.
- Can the children name the colors of the small shapes?

Children's Books

Of Colors and Things by
    Tana Hoban
*What Makes a
Rainbow?* by Betty Ann
    Schwartz

Susan Oldham Hill, Lakeland, FL

Blue, Blue Sky

LEARNING OBJECTIVES

The children will:
1. Learn to match the colors of the rainbow.
2. Develop their small motor skills by blotting and painting.

Materials

drawing of a rainbow
with the colors in
the correct order:
red, orange, yellow,
green, blue, violet
drawing of a rainbow
with the uncolored
bands marked in
pencil
fingerpaint paper
blue fingerpaint
tagboard
tissues
glue
smocks
scissors (adult only)
pencil

VOCABULARY

clouds	color names (red,	crumple	rainbow
	orange, yellow,	fingerpaint	
	green, blue,		
	violet)		

PREPARATION

● Make a drawing of a rainbow with the bands of color in the typical color-wheel order.
● Cut 5" x 10" rectangles from tagboard. Pencil in a rainbow with six ½" bands. Cut away excess tagboard so that only the rainbow shape remains.

WHAT TO DO

1. Put a sprinkle of water on the tables to hold the fingerpaint paper in place. Ask the children to put on smocks. Set out blue fingerpaint for the children.
2. Ask the children to move the paint around across the whole page with their fingers and hands. Encourage them to swirl the paint around to look like clouds.
3. Give each child a tissue and ask him to crumple it up. Show them how to blot areas of the paper while the paint is still wet to make clouds.
4. While the paint dries, give each child a blank tagboard rainbow. Show them the drawing of the rainbow with the colors in the correct order. Ask the children to color their own rainbow.
5. The next day, when the paintings are dry, return the rainbows to the children to glue onto their cloud paintings.

ASSESSMENT

To assess the children's learning, consider the following:
● Can each child match the cut-apart bands of the rainbow to the correct bands on the drawing?
● Can the children name the colors in the rainbow?

Susan Oldham Hill, Lakeland, FL

Children's Books

Rainbow Fish by
Marcus Pfister
Rain Drop Splash by
Alvin Tresselt
*What Makes a
Rainbow?* by
Betty Ann Schwartz

Color Blending

4+

The children will:

1. Experiment with color.
2. Discover how colors mix to form new colors.
3. Describe their findings to other children.

Materials

red, yellow, blue, black, and white paint
white paper
cotton swabs or paintbrushes

VOCABULARY

blend	palette	secondary color	shade
mix	primary color		

PREPARATION

● Create a "palette page" to photocopy for each child. Trace three medium circles in separate corners on the horizontal page. Label these "Red," "Yellow," and "Blue." Trace two small circles on opposite sides of the page. Label these "Black" and "White." Trace seven to nine small circles for paint mixing.

WHAT TO DO

1. Explain to the children that colors blend with others to make new colors. Tell them that adding white to a color will make it lighter and black will darken it.
2. Give each child a palette page and place a dollop of each paint color in the appropriate circle. Let them combine bits of colors in the blank circles to see what results.
3. Encourage the children to share what they see happening as they mix. Talk with them about the colors they create, using color names.
4. Allow plenty of time for experimentation. Let the papers dry thoroughly.

ASSESSMENT

To assess the children's learning, consider the following:

● Ask children what they think about the transformation of colors. Can the children use color names to define the colors they create? (For example, "That looks purple-y.")
● Can the children describe the results of combinations they make? ("What do red and yellow make?" "Red and yellow make orange.")

Jaclyn Miller, Mishawaka, IN

Children's Books

The Colors of Us by Karen Katz
Purple, Green, and Yellow by Robert Munsch

Let's Cut Some Colors!

4+

LEARNING OBJECTIVES

The children will:

1. Recognize and name colors.
2. Practice making choices of pictures to cut or tear from magazines.
3. Follow directions.
4. Develop their small motor coordination.
5. Discuss their collage with their friends.

Materials

a variety of magazines
(fashion, sports,
fitness, family)
construction paper
child-safe scissors
glue or paste
markers

VOCABULARY

collage	glue	names of unfamiliar
color names	magazine	objects children
cut	paste	choose for their
	tear	collage

PREPARATION

- Assemble and arrange magazines in an area where children can select pictures that appeal to them.
- Place child-safe scissors and glue in a convenient location.

WHAT TO DO

1. Review colors with the children.
2. Select a color of the day or week to feature in the activity.
3. Invite the children to choose a magazine and find pictures of objects that are the color of the day.
4. Allow the children to cut or tear the pictures from the magazine and paste them on the construction paper.
5. When everyone is finished, invite them to come together in a large group. Ask for volunteers to name and discuss the pictures they chose.

ASSESSMENT

To assess the children's learning, consider the following:

- Can the children identify objects according to the chosen color? (Note each child's ability to follow directions and his comfort with discussing his collage with others.)
- Are the children displaying an age-appropriate development of small motor skills as they cut or tear pictures from magazines?

Children's Books

Blue Hat, Green Hat by
Sandra Boynton
*What Color Is It?/¿Qué
color es éste?* by the
editors of the American
Heritage Dictionary

Song

"De Colores" from
Songs of Our World by
Raffi

Margery Kranyik Fermino, West Roxbury, MA

Building with Color

3+

LEARNING OBJECTIVES

The children will:

1. Identify colors.
2. Build creatively.
3. Develop oral language skills.

Materials

colored plastic cups, plates, and bowls
colorful building blocks

VOCABULARY

bottom	building	top	tower
build	color		

WHAT TO DO

1. Demonstrate how cups, bowls, and plates can be stacked on top of one another to create a structure or building.
2. Invite the children to use the materials to build and construct various buildings and towers.
3. Suggest that the children to talk about the colors they are working with as they create the buildings.
4. Encourage each child to show her finished building to a friend and name its colors before knocking it down.

TEACHER-TO-TEACHER TIP

- Colored plastic tableware is available at your local discount or party store.

ASSESSMENT

To assess the children's learning, consider the following:

- Challenge the children to work together, taking turns to build a structure out of colorful plastic pieces of tableware. Can the children identify the colors of the pieces of tableware they add to the structure?
- Can the children sort the cups, plates, and bowls they used to build their structure, according to color?

Children's Books

Mouse Paint by Ellen Stoll Walsh
My Crayons Talk by Patricia Hubbard
Sorting by David Kirkby
White Rabbit's Color Book by Alan Baker

Mary J. Murray, Mazomanie, WI

Harold & the Purple Crayon 3+

LEARNING OBJECTIVES

The children will:

1. Hear a story about drawing and coloring.
2. Express themselves, using crayons as the medium.
3. Talk about their drawings.

Materials

Harold and the Purple
   Crayon by Crockett
   Johnson (or any
   book from the
   series)
butcher paper or
   newsprint, one
   piece for each child
crayons in all colors
easel or wall

VOCABULARY

crayon	draw	imagination	purple
dark	express	light	story

WHAT TO DO

1. Read Harold and the Purple Crayon (or another book from the series) with the children.
2. Give the children a piece of paper. Show them the crayons. Talk about how Harold used just one crayon in his book and created a whole story with it.
3. Tell the children that they are going to create their own stories by only using one crayon.
4. Each child chooses one crayon. Invite the children to spread out on the floor or at a table, wherever they are comfortable. Play soft music in the background.
5. Have the children draw whatever they wish using their chosen colors.
6. When they are finished, regroup near the easel or wall space. Choose a volunteer to come up and attach his paper on the easel or tape to the wall for easy presentation.
7. The children take turns telling and sharing their stories. Help them label their papers as mentioned above (____and the ____ Crayon) and dictate as much as they can. Display the finished projects with the title "The Adventures of [class name] and Their Crayons!"

ASSESSMENT

To assess the children's learning, consider the following:

● Watch the children draw during free art and observe whether they tell a story as they draw.
● Can the children describe the steps involved in building or drawing an object, as they are progressing through those steps?

Shelley Hoster, Norcross, GA

Children's Books

Chicka Chicka Boom
Boom by Bill Martin, Jr.
My Crayons Talk by
Patricia Hubbard

Mary Wore Her Red Dress 3+

LEARNING OBJECTIVES

The children will:

1. Participate in a song about colors.
2. Feel proud about what they are wearing.
3. Learn the names of colors.
4. Take turns looking at and talking about the classroom book.

Materials

Mary Wore Her Red Dress and Henry Wore His Green Sneakers by Merle Peek

photo of each child

binder

plastic page protector sleeves

VOCABULARY

| author | clothing items (pants, bibs, shirt, dress, stocking, socks, shoes, hat) | color names descriptors (striped, polka dot, flowered) | illustrator |

PREPARATION

● Take photos of each child with a digital camera and print them on a color printer.

WHAT TO DO

1. Read the book *Mary Wore Her Red Dress and Henry Wore His Green Sneakers* by Merle Peek to the children.
2. Reread the book and ask the children to help say the words. Invite the children to act out the story.
3. Explain that the children are going to make their own book, and that they will be the authors, illustrators, and characters in the book.
4. Attach photos of each child to different sheets of paper. Type or handwrite under each child's picture "[Child's name] is wearing [color] [clothing item]." Have the child help choose what he wants to write about. Allow for creative license. The children may want to say "truck shirt," "car shoes," "striped shirt," "blue jeans," or "flower pants."
5. Use a binder or string to collect the children's pages together into a book.

ASSESSMENT

To assess the children's learning, consider the following:

● Did the children participate in at least part of the song/rhyme and help tell the story?
● Can the children indicate what they are wearing and name the color of what they are wearing?
● Can the children discuss the characters in *Mary Wore Her Red Dress and Henry Wore His Green Sneakers*?

Children's Books

Pinkalicious by Victoria Kann and Elizabeth Kann

The Principal's New Clothes by Stephanie Calmenson

Sandra Nagel, White Lake, MI

What Makes the Color Green? 3+

LEARNING OBJECTIVES

The children will:

1. Learn that yellow and blue make green.
2. Recognize the colors yellow, blue, and green.
3. Improve comprehension skills and their ability to retell a story.
4. Recognize circles.

Materials

yellow and blue
  playdough
snack-size resealable
  bags
*Little Blue and Little
  Yellow* by Leo Lionni

VOCABULARY

blue	green	mix	yellow

PREPARATION

- A day in advance, send a note home to families asking them to dress their child in yellow, blue, or green the next day. Explain that the class will be learning about mixing blue and yellow to make green.
- Roll yellow and blue playdough into tiny balls, making enough for each child to have one of each color. If possible, roll enough for each child to be able to take one of each home in a resealable bag.

WHAT TO DO

1. Tell the children that you would like them to help you tell the story you are going to read. Tell them every time you say, "little blue" or "little yellow" they should hold up a playdough ball of that color.
2. Give each child one ball of yellow playdough and one ball of blue playdough.
3. Read the story *Little Blue and Little Yellow* to the children. After little blue and little yellow hug in the story, ask the children to squish their playdough balls together until they become single green balls. (Let them "discover" this.)

ASSESSMENT

To assess the children's learning, consider the following:

- Can the children identify and differentiate between yellow, blue, and green?
- Can the children describe what happened when little blue and little yellow mixed together?

Holly Dzierzanowski, Brenham, TX

Children's Books

A Color of His Own by
  Leo Lionni
*Little Blue and Little
  Yellow* by Leo Lionni
*One Fish, Two Fish, Red
  Fish, Blue Fish* by
  Dr. Seuss

Caps for Sale

LEARNING OBJECTIVES

The children will:
1. Sort caps by color.
2. Identify the colors red, brown, gray, and blue.

Materials

Caps for Sale by Esphyr Slobodkina
box
approximately five each of red, gray, brown, and blue baseball caps (ask the children's families for loaners or donations)
one checked cap

VOCABULARY

bottom   monkey   peddler   top
cap

PREPARATION

- Put all of the caps into a large box.
- In advance, ask a family member or another teacher to come to class to play the role of the peddler in *Caps for Sale*.

WHAT TO DO

1. Read the story *Caps for Sale* to the children.
2. Show the children the box of caps. Name the colors of the caps. Encourage the children to sort the caps by color. Ask the children to say the name of each color cap as it is placed in the correct pile.
3. Give each child one cap. Ask each child to tell you the color of the cap.
4. Reread the story. This time have the children put the caps on the "peddler's" head at the appropriate time.
5. Encourage the children to pretend to be monkeys at appropriate moments in the story.

ASSESSMENT

To assess the children's learning, consider the following:
- Set out all the hats and challenge the children to sort them by color.
- Can the children identify the colors of the different hats?

Children's Books

Brown Bear, Brown Bear, What Do You See? by Bill Martin, Jr.
One Fish, Two Fish, Red Fish, Blue Fish by Dr. Seuss

Karyn F. Everham, Fort Myers, FL

Colorful Honey

4+

LEARNING OBJECTIVES

The children will:
1. Learn about bees and honey production.
2. Develop color awareness.

Materials

four or five different
   types/colors of
   honey (ask families
   for donations)
paper plates
The Honey Makers by
   Gail Gibbons

VOCABULARY

amber	golden	honeybee	lighter
brown	hive	larvae	yellow
darker			

PREPARATION

● Place the honey in clear plastic containers and close lids tightly.
● Arrange a few drops of each type of honey on a paper plate, keeping them far
   enough apart so that the small color pools do not mix.
   Safety Note: Check for any food allergies before doing this activity.

WHAT TO DO

1. Read *The Honey Makers* and then
   show the children the containers of
   honey.
2. Point out and explore the color
   gradations, perhaps using paper and
   pastels to illustrate the range of
   colors.
3. Allow the children to smell, touch,
   and taste the honey samples on
   paper plates.

Children's Books

The Big Honey Hunt
by Stan Berenstain and
Jan Berenstain
Honey...Honey...Lion!
by Jan Brett
The Honey Makers by
Gail Gibbons

Song

Sing "I'm Bringing
Home a Baby
Bumblebee" with the
children.

TEACHER-TO-TEACHER TIP

● Dilute a honey sample to 20% honey and 80% water. This is the strength of
   the nectar that bees extract from flowers, and which they then process into
   honey in the hive.

ASSESSMENT

To assess the children's learning, consider the following:
● Do the children display an understanding of where honey comes from?
● Can the children describe the color and flavor of honey?

Patrick Mitchell, Yagoto, Nagoya, Japan

Kitten Coloring

LEARNING OBJECTIVES

The children will:
1. Identify primary colors.
2. Identify the resulting color from mixing two primary colors.
3. List everyday objects associated with a particular color.
4. Talk about their painting in a language-experience story.

Materials

easels or tables
newspaper
warm soapy water
paper towels
The Color Kittens by
    Margaret Wise
    Brown
washable tempera
    paint in basic
    primary colors
brushes
large sheets of paper
    cut in the shape of
    kittens or cats
pictures of everyday
    items
chart paper

VOCABULARY

brushes   color names   paint

PREPARATION

● Before children arrive, cover the work area with newspaper and provide warm soapy water and paper towels.
● Post pictures of everyday items in a variety of colors near the work area.

WHAT TO DO

1. Gather the children together and take a "picture walk" through *The Color Kittens*. A picture walk involves no reading but lots of discussion. Discuss what the children see the kittens doing, and talk about the colors the kittens are making. Then read the book, stopping to let the children "read" the colors that are made.
2. After reading, invite the children to paint on their kitten-shaped paper. Some children will want to use just one primary color. Engage the children in a discussion of what else, in the everyday world, would be that color. Encourage the children who mix colors to talk about how they came up with their results. Refer to the posted pictures if a child appears stuck.
3. Follow up with a language-experience story, giving each child an opportunity to describe the colors he used in his painting and what it represents to him. For example, "Simon painted with red. Simon says his mom's coat is red."

ASSESSMENT

To assess the children's learning, consider the following:
● Can the children identify the colors they used?
● Can the children identify various items in the posted pictures, and name the colors of those items?

Children's Books

The Color Kittens by
Margaret Wise Brown
Three Little Kittens by
Paul Galdone

Carol Mayer, Sparta, IL

My Crayons Talk

4+

LEARNING OBJECTIVES

The children will:
1. Listen to a story about crayons.
2. Create their own pages to put in a class book.

Materials

My Crayons Talk by
  Patricia Hubbard
paper
crayons
chart paper

VOCABULARY

color names	draw	say
crayon	imagine	talk

WHAT TO DO

1. Gather the children for story time. Read the story and talk about the things that each color said or drew.
2. Pass the crayons around the circle and have each child choose one.
3. Say, for example, "I see you have chosen blue. If you were a blue crayon, what would you say?"
4. Write their responses down on chart paper.
5. Invite the children to draw a picture with their chosen color. Have each child dictate a sentence or two about the picture and write it underneath the drawing.
6. Attach the children's pictures together in book fashion and read it to the children afterwards. Place the book in the class library for future reading.

ASSESSMENT

To assess the children's learning, consider the following:

● When shown a color, can the children name objects that are the same color?

● When drawing, do the children use appropriate colors (such as blue for sky or water, green for grass) to represent real objects? Do they use colors in a creative way?

● If the children use nontraditional colors in a drawing, such as drawing purple grass, can the children articulate why they did so?

Shelley Hoster, Norcross, GA

Children's Books

Dog's Colorful Day by
  Emma Dodd
Elmer by David McKee
Planting a Rainbow by
  Lois Ehlert

Color Pops

3+

LEARNING OBJECTIVES

The children will:
1. Recognize different colors.
2. Begin to recognize letters and names of colors (older children only).

Materials

construction paper
craft sticks

VOCABULARY

color names   mixing   trade

PREPARATION

- Cut out several circles from each color of construction paper.
- Write the name of the color on the circle; then attach each circle to a craft stick.

WHAT TO DO

1. Begin by reviewing all colors with the children. Have the children name each color as you hold up each color stick. Ask the children what two colors make other colors. For example, "What two colors make the color green?"
2. You might want to make enough so that each child has one of each color. Call out a color and have the children hold up the correct one. Ask each child to hold up a specific color.
3. Have the children trade colors with each other.
4. Encourage older children to read color names. Also, ask the older children to identify the letter their color starts with. For example, "Hold up the color that begins with the letter R."

ASSESSMENT

To assess the children's learning, consider the following:
- Can the children identify the various colors, letters, and words discussed during the activity?

Children's Books

Dog's Colorful Day by Emma Dodd
Mouse Paint by Ellen Stoll Walsh
White Rabbit's Colorful Book by Alan Baker

Hilary Romig, Las Cruces, NM

Circle Color Game

LEARNING OBJECTIVES

The children will:

1. Reinforce learning of colors.
2. Experience social interactions.
3. Make decisions within a time limit.

Materials

solid-color objects
(toys, strings of
beads, and so on)

VOCABULARY

circle   color names   friend

PREPARATION

● Collect at least twice as many objects as the number of children in the class.

WHAT TO DO

1. Put a selection of colored objects into the center of the circle.
2. Teach the children the following rhyme:

   My Friends by Anne Adeney
   I have a friend,
   And _____ is her name.
   I will give her something (color name)
   In the circle color game.

3. Ask a child to pick another child, choose a color, and chant the rhyme. The child should go into the center, choose an object of the correct color, and give it to her friend to hold. As the child is doing so, all the children should chant the rhyme, for example: "Dylan has a friend, and Carly is her name. He will give her something blue in the circle color game."
4. The child who has been given the object sings the rhyme next.
5. Continue until each child has both given and received an object.

TEACHER-TO-TEACHER TIP

● Ask the last child chosen to start the game the next time.

Children's Books

Color Dance by
Ann Jonas
Color Farm by
Lois Ehlert
Maisy's Color Collection
by Lucy Cousins

ASSESSMENT

To assess the children's learning, consider the following:

● Review color names with the children. Are they able to identify and differentiate between the various colors?

Anne Adeney, Plymouth, England, United Kingdom

Color Circle

3+

LEARNING OBJECTIVES

The children will:
1. Learn to recognize colors.
2. Identify colors by name.

Materials

masking tape
construction paper
(red, orange, yellow,
green, blue, purple)
scissors (adult only)
stapler (adult only)
color die
crayons (red, orange,
yellow, green, blue,
purple)

VOCABULARY
color names   headband

PREPARATION
- Use masking tape to mark off a large circle on the rug.
- Make different colors of headbands using 18" x 24" construction paper, folding a 3" wide strip into a 1½" band. Staple to fit the average child's head.
- Make a 4" cube from a small box. Cut a square of construction paper to fit on each side, using the colors red, orange, yellow, green, blue, and purple.

WHAT TO DO
1. Give each child a headband (use a variety of colors). Ask the children to sit around the edge of the circle, but not too close to one another.
2. Give one child the cube to roll and ask them all to call out the color showing on top of the die. Choose a starting point in the circle of children, and ask the first person wearing that color headband to sit in the circle.
3. Ask that child to roll the die again and name the color showing on top of the die. Ask the first child wearing that color to sit in the circle.
4. Repeat until the circle is full.

ASSESSMENT
To assess the children's learning, consider the following:
- Can the children name the colors of the headbands?

Susan Oldham Hill, Lakeland, FL

Children's Books

Colors Everywhere by
Tana Hoban
*Is It Red? Is It Yellow? Is
It Blue?* by Tana Hoban
Mouse Paint by
Ellen Stoll Walsh
Red Is Best by
Kathy Stinson

Color Search

LEARNING OBJECTIVES

The children will:

1. Identify the color of a paper correctly.
2. Learn a chant.
3. Match the color of a paper to an object.

Materials

construction paper in each color to be taught

small objects that match construction paper colors

VOCABULARY

color names   match   search

PREPARATION

● Gather materials in the middle of the circle or group area. Make sure you have enough paper to give one to each child.

WHAT TO DO

1. Review the colors you have studied by showing the children the paper one at a time. Give each child a piece of construction paper and ask him to identify the color (children may have the same color).
2. Explain to the children that when they hear the color they are holding, they should search for something in the room that is the same color.
3. Chant, "Tell me can you find it, tell me can you find it, tell me can you find it: green."
4. The children with green papers locate a green object and hold it up for all to see.
5. Repeat the chant, encouraging the children to join in on all but the color word. Chant with a different color until each child has had a turn to search for a match.
6. Switch papers and play again.

TEACHER-TO-TEACHER TIP

● This activity can be done using shapes or shapes and colors together.

ASSESSMENT

To assess the children's learning, consider the following:

● Can the children accurately identify the color of each paper?
● Can the children match objects to the colored paper without assistance?
● Are the children able to repeat the chant?

Children's Books

Brown Bear, Brown Bear, What Do You See? by Eric Carle
Color Farm by Lois Ehlert
Color Zoo by Lois Ehlert
Mouse Paint by Ellen Stoll Walsh
Planting a Rainbow by Lois Ehlert

Debbie Vilardi, Commack, NY

Color Watch

3+

LEARNING OBJECTIVES

The children will:
1. Learn about colors.
2. Learn the meaning of the words "under" and "on."

Materials

Brown Bear, Brown Bear, What Do You See? by Bill Martin, Jr.

VOCABULARY

around   on   spot   under

WHAT TO DO

1. Read the story to the children.
2. Select a child to be the bear.
3. The other children ask her a question about a color in the classroom. For example, "Brown bear, brown bear, what yellow object do you see?"
4. Ask the bear to look *around* the room, *under* the table, *on* the wall and the ceiling. The bear then points to an object in the classroom and says, "I see a yellow cup on the table."
5. Repeat the question with different colors and continue the game with other children taking turns as the bear.

ASSESSMENT

To assess the children's learning, consider the following:
● Can the children name the colors of various items?
● Given an object, can a child find another object of the same color in the classroom?

Children's Books

Chicka Chicka, 1, 2, 3 by Bill Martin, Jr.
Mouse Paint by Ellen Stoll Walsh
One Fish Two Fish Red Fish Blue Fish by Dr. Seuss

Shyamala Shanmugasundaram, Nerul, Navi Mumbai, India

Hurry Up! Pick One Up!

3+

LEARNING OBJECTIVES

The children will:

1. Identify colors.
2. Improve their oral language skills.

Materials

six or eight different colored baskets or gift bags with handles
classroom objects of various colors

VOCABULARY

bag	color	hurry	pick
basket			

WHAT TO DO

1. Sing the children's favorite color song as they pass the baskets around the circle.
2. When the song ends, whoever is holding a basket stands up.
3. The children chant, "What color do you have, [child's name]?" The child responds by naming the color of her basket.
4. The children reply by chanting, "Hurry up, pick one up."
5. The child searches and finds an object of the same color to place inside her basket.
6. Meanwhile, the children repeat the chant with the remaining children holding baskets.
7. As soon as each participant finds an object, she hurries back to the circle area with her basket.
8. Once all children have returned, invite the children to talk about the object they found and then place the items in the center of the circle.
9. Repeat the activity several times until all children have had one or more turns.

TEACHER-TO-TEACHER TIPS

- Purchase different colored baskets inexpensively during post-holiday sales or find them at nearby rummage sales.
- As an alternative, attach a large colored ribbon or paper shape to plain brown wicker baskets to designate colors.

ASSESSMENT

To assess the children's learning, consider the following:

- Can the children name the colors of their baskets and describe the objects they find?
- After the activity, invite each child to pick up one or more objects from the center of the circle area. Display the baskets in the center of the circle. Can each child name the color of her object and then place it in the matching colored basket?

Children's Books

Colors Everywhere by Tana Hoban
Color Zoo by Lois Ehlert
Living Color by Steve Jenkins

Mary J. Murray, Mazomanie, WI

Leaves Are Falling

3+

LEARNING OBJECTIVES
The children will:
1. Identify color of leaves.
2. Sort leaves by color.

Materials

real or paper leaves in fall colors (orange, red, yellow, brown) and green leaves

large piece of fabric or material (tablecloth or sheet)

two baskets or boxes large enough to hold the leaves

VOCABULARY

brown	green	orange	yellow
fall	leaves	red	

PREPARATION
- Label one basket "Green" and the other "Orange, Red, Yellow, and Brown."

WHAT TO DO
1. Talk about the colors of leaves in the fall.
2. Show children the real or paper leaves and ask what they notice about the colors.
3. Tell the children that they are going to make the fall leaves fall! Show them the baskets and explain that after the leaves fall, they are going to sort them by color and place them in the appropriate basket.
4. Put the baskets on opposite sides of the circle.
5. Have children stand around the large cloth and hold onto the edges. Pile the leaves onto the top of the cloth and help the children lift the cloth up and down to toss the leaves into the air.
6. While they are tossing the leaves, ask children to call out colors they see.
7. Say, "When I count to three, we are going to let go of the cloth. When the cloth falls to the ground, collect the leaves one at a time and take them to the basket that matches their color."
8. Count to three and help the children drop the cloth and sort the leaves.
9. When all of the leaves are collected, consider looking through the collected leaves or repeating the activity.

ASSESSMENT
To assess the children's learning, consider the following:
- Can each child identify the main colors on three leaves? Can they match the leaves to baskets of the same colors?

Cassandra Reigel Whetstone, Folsom, CA

Children's Books

Fletcher and the Falling Leaves by Julia Rawlinson
Mouse's First Fall by Lauren Thompson
Why Do Leaves Change Color? by Betsy Maestro

Swatch Match

LEARNING OBJECTIVES

The children will:

1. Explore and talk about different colors.
2. Match paint swatches by color.

Materials

paint swatches from paint store (two of each shade)
poster board
Velcro
bag or basket (decorated with paint swatches, if desired)

VOCABULARY

color   color names   match   swatch

PREPARATION

- Cut apart paint swatches if there is more than one color on a sheet.
- Make a Color Match board by gluing one of each color pair to the poster board in a row or column, leaving space in between each one.
- Glue or attach a Velcro dot next to each swatch, leaving room for children to attach the other swatch. Glue or attach the opposite side of the Velcro dots to the other swatches.
- Place the other color in each pair in the bag or basket.

WHAT TO DO

1. Place the poster in the circle or group time area. Gather the children and talk about the colors they see on the poster.
2. Have them take turns drawing out a color swatch from the bag and see if they can name the color.
3. Ask them to find the match or "friend" of their color and place it on the poster board.
4. Continue playing until all the colors have been matched. Display in the math area for children to do independently.

ASSESSMENT

To assess the children's learning, consider the following:

- When shown an object, can each child name its color?
- Can each child match like-colored objects in the classroom?

Shelley Hoster, Norcross, GA

Children's Books

Cat's Colors by Jane Cabrera
Is It Red? Is It Yellow? Is It Blue? by Tana Hoban
Of Colors and Things by Tana Hoban

What Color Are You?

LEARNING OBJECTIVES

The children will:
1. Identify colors.
2. Develop listening skills.
3. Follow directions to complete physical tasks.

Materials

die-cut circles in red, yellow, orange, green, and blue clothespins, safety pins, or masking tape

VOCABULARY

blue	green	red	yellow
clothespins	orange	tape	

WHAT TO DO

1. Hold up the die-cut circles and have the children identify the colors they see.
2. Give each child a circle, and pin or tape these circles onto the children's clothes. (**Safety Note**: If using safety pins, be sure only adults pin the circles to the children's clothes.) Ask the children to name their colors.
3. Give instructions to the children based on the color of their circle. For example, you can say, "Reds, stand up. Blues, touch your nose. Yellows, pat your heads. Greens, hop on one foot," and so on.
4. Try varying the instructions to make the actions more complex. For example, combine instructions for multiple colors by saying, "Reds and blues, clap your hands." Alternatively, give multi-step directions and say, "Greens, close your eyes and touch your toes."

POEM

A Rainbow of Colors by Laura Wynkoop

Red is the color of a fire truck.
Orange is the color of a juicy fruit.
Yellow is the color of a baby duck.

Green is the color of a new spring shoot.
Blue is the color of the sparkling sea.
A rainbow of colors is all around me.

TEACHER-TO-TEACHER TIP

- Use color-based instructions to return the children to their seats or to transition to the next activity.

ASSESSMENT

To assess the children's learning, consider the following:
- Are the children able to name the colors of the circles?
- Can the children follow one-step directions based on their colors?
- Can they follow multi-step directions based on their colors?

Children's Books

Butterfly Butterfly: A Book of Colors by Petr Horacek
A Red Train: A Colors Book by Bernette Ford

Laura Wynkoop, San Dimas, CA

Who Do You See?

LEARNING OBJECTIVES

The children will:
1. Identify colors.
2. Learn the names of their classmates.

Materials

no materials necessary

VOCABULARY

color names (red, yellow, blue, green, orange, purple, black, white)

direction words (clockwise, right)

WHAT TO DO

1. Sit with the children in a circle.
2. The activity moves clockwise around the circle. Each child identifies the person sitting to her right using the color of that person's shirt and her name.
3. The children help to start by asking, "Teacher, teacher, who do you see?"

4. Reply with, "I see [color of child's shirt] [child's name] sitting next to me." For instance, say, "I see red Matthew sitting next to me."
5. Everyone then asks, "Red Matthew, red Matthew, who do you see?"
6. Matthew would reply, for example, with, "I see blue Megan sitting next to me."
7. This continues until the last child identifies you. ("I see green Miss Smith sitting next to me.")

TEACHER-TO-TEACHER TIP

● This is a great activity to do at the beginning of the year to help the children become familiar with each other's names. In a new class, children may need help naming the child sitting next to them.

ASSESSMENT

To assess the children's learning, consider the following:
● Can the children properly identify and name colors?
● Can the children identify their classmates by name?

Children's Books

Brown Bear, Brown Bear, What Do You See? by Bill Martin, Jr.
Chicka Chicka, 1, 2, 3 by Bill Martin, Jr.
Polar Bear, Polar Bear, What Do You Hear? by Bill Martin, Jr and Eric Carle

Janet Hammond, Mount Laurel, NJ

Color Band Connections

LEARNING OBJECTIVES

The children will:
1. Practice matching colors.
2. Work with other children to create chains.

Materials

a set of crayons in red, orange, yellow, green, blue, purple, brown, black, and white

a set of color flash cards in red, orange, yellow, green, blue, purple, brown, black, and white

12" x 3" construction paper in red, orange, yellow, green, blue, purple, brown, black, and white

stapler (adult only)

Children's Books

Colors Everywhere by Tana Hoban

Look at Rainbow Colors by Rena K. Kirkpatrick

Mr. Rabbit and the Lovely Present by Charlotte Zolotow

Red, Blue, Yellow Shoe by Tana Hoban

VOCABULARY

| chain | color names (red, orange, yellow, green, blue, violet) | matching | wristband |

PREPARATION

● Fold the 12" x 3" strips of colored construction paper into bands 1 ½" wide.

WHAT TO DO

1. Ask each child to choose two bands of different colors. Staple one loosely around each wrist.
2. Ask a child to start the "chain" by choosing another child who has the same color on one wrist. The child with a matching color band comes up to hold hands with the first child.
3. Next, the second child chooses another child whose band matches the other wristband. Continue until everyone has matched with another person's wristband color.
4. Repeat with a new starting child to make a different chain.

SONG

Color Chain by Susan Oldham Hill

(Tune: Second verse of "She'll Be Comin' 'Round the Mountain")

Red holds hands with red, now,
Blue holds hands with blue,
Yellow holds hands with yellow,
And I hold hands with you!

Purple with purple, green with green,
And I hold hands with you!
Orange with orange, brown with brown,
'Til our chain is through!

ASSESSMENT

To assess the children's learning, consider the following:

● Ask the children, one by one, to match the crayons and the color flash cards. This is a good time to practice naming the colors as well.

> Susan Oldham Hill, Lakeland, FL

My Cat's Favorite Color

LEARNING OBJECTIVES

The children will:
1. Identify and name various colors.
2. Sort objects by color.
3. Match the colors with other like colors.

Materials

Cat's Colors by Jane
    Cabrera
construction paper in
    several colors
stapler
black marker
magazines
scissors

VOCABULARY

| earth | floating | snooze | swoop |
| favorite | petals | soar | tangle |

PREPARATION

- Make one large cat die-cut in each of the following colors: red, blue, yellow, purple, orange, white, brown, green, pink, and black. Cut out a 4" x 6" squares for each color. Staple the squares to the back of each cat to make a pocket.
- Write the color name on the large cat in black marker.
- Make two to four small die-cut cats per color and laminate for durability.
- Gather magazines and scissors.

WHAT TO DO

1. Read Cat's Colors by Jane Cabrera.
2. Give each child a small die-cut cat.
3. Once you have given all the children a color, ask them to find the other children with the same cat color.
4. After children have found their group, give them their large cat. Inform them that they will be finding their cat's favorite color things. In other words, they will be looking for things in the magazine that are the color of their cat.
5. Give children time to find at least five pictures and place them in the pocket of their cat.
6. Once everyone has done this, regroup and share the color of their cat and the things that they found.
7. Gather pictures and color cats and display them on the class bulletin board by color groups.

Children's Books

I Love Colors! by
Hans Wilhelm
White Rabbit's Color
Book by Alan Baker

ASSESSMENT

To assess the children's learning, consider the following:
- Can the children match color words to color samples?
- Provide a group of objects of different colors and ask the children to name the color of each object. Can they sort the objects by color?

Quazonia Quarles, Newark, DE

Color Picnic

3+

LEARNING OBJECTIVES

The children will:

1. Improve oral language skills.
2. Identify colors.
3. Practice counting skills.

Materials

colorful picnic items such as colored plastic plates, cups, bowls, napkins, silverware, empty juice boxes and food containers, and artificial fruit
picnic basket
blanket

VOCABULARY

blanket	colors	picnic basket	silverware
bowl	food	plate	

PREPARATION

- Place the materials inside the picnic basket.
- Fold the blanket or tablecloth and place it inside or beneath the picnic basket.

WHAT TO DO

1. Invite two or more children to carry the picnic basket to an open area of the classroom.
2. Help the children place the blanket on the floor.
3. Have the children remove each item and identify it by name and color.
4. Invite the children to have a color picnic with the supplies. Ask them questions about the colors of the different items as they play.
5. Ask the children to place the items back in the basket and fold up the blanket when they are finished.

TEACHER-TO-TEACHER TIP

- Place a different assortment of food in the basket each day so children will want to try this activity over and over. You might also put two teddy bears near the basket so that children can have a "teddy bear picnic."

ASSESSMENT

To assess the children's learning, consider the following:

- Listen as children talk about the items and colors as they display the materials on the blanket. Can each child take an item from the basket, say its color aloud, and then display the item on the blanket?

Mary J. Murray, Mazomanie, WI

Children's Books

Eating Fractions by Bruce McMillan
Food for Thought by Saxton Freymann
Sam's Sandwich by David Pelham
The Sandwich That Max Made by Marcia Vaughan
Teddy Bear Picnic by Jimmy Kennedy
Zak's Lunch by Margie Palatini

Dressing the Mascot

LEARNING OBJECTIVES

The children will:
1. Reinforce their color awareness.
2. Match colors by name or picture.
3. Improve basic life skills such as fastening clothes.

Materials

two (or more, if available) large rag dolls, boy and girl doll clothes in various colors

VOCABULARY

button	hook and eye	Velcro	zipper
color names	snap		

PREPARATION

- Collect a large assortment of doll clothes, in basic colors for younger children and shades of colors for older ones. Family members are often more than willing to sew or knit for this project. Select clothing with an assortment of button, zip, snap, hook and eye, and Velcro fastenings.

WHAT TO DO

1. Hopefully you will end up with a large box of clothes, which you can ask a child to sort into colors or use to dress dolls in the "color of the day."
2. Encourage the children to follow instructions and dress the dolls in various ways by saying, "Please dress one in orange and brown clothes," or "Please dress this one in something red, something yellow, something blue, and something green."
3. Invite the children to play with the different clothes to practice using different fastenings.

TEACHER-TO-TEACHER TIP

- Many boys have been encouraged from an early age not to play with dolls. Giving the rag dolls names and referring to them as "class mascots" or a similar word will help overcome this problem.

ASSESSMENT

To assess the children's learning, consider the following:
- Encourage the children to pick the correct color when asked to find the blue clothes. Does each child still need a pictorial clue to help him?
- Can the children identify the clothes' fastenings by name?
- Are the children exhibiting age-appropriate small motor skills when using the different fastenings, such as zippers and snaps?

Children's Books

Ella Sarah Gets Dressed by Margaret Chodos-Irvine
Maddie Wants New Clothes by Louise Leblanc

Anne Adeney, Plymouth, England, United Kingdom

Shoe Store

3+

LEARNING OBJECTIVES

The children will:
1. Match like shoes.
2. Identify colors.
3. Improve social skills.

Materials

six or more pairs of
   different colored
   shoes
six or more shoeboxes
"Shoe Store" sign

VOCABULARY

color	shoe	size
fit	shoebox	wear

PREPARATION
- Place all the shoes in the shoeboxes with mismatched shoes together.
- Cover each box with its lid.
- Display the boxes on the floor along with the "Shoe Store" sign.

WHAT TO DO
1. Invite the children to come to the "shoe store."
2. Have the children open the boxes and identify the colors of both shoes inside each box.
3. The children place all the shoes on the floor and match pairs of shoes together.
4. Have the children place a pair of matching shoes inside each shoebox and put the lid on top.
5. When they are finished, the children may offer to "sell" a pair of shoes to their classmates.
6. As an option, include play money, a toy cash register, ruler for measuring feet, bags to place purchased shoes in, and so on.

TEACHER-TO-TEACHER TIP
- Have children place mismatched shoes back in the boxes before leaving the "Shoe Store" so the game is ready for the next person.

ASSESSMENT
To assess the children's learning, consider the following:
- Can the children name the colors of each individual shoe?
- Invite the children to try on pairs of shoes and walk around the room to find objects of the same color as the shoes.
- Have children line up the shoes end to end. Can the children walk along the line of shoes and name each shoe color as they walk?

Children's Books

Big Ones, Little Ones
   by Tana Hoban
Red, Blue, Yellow Shoe
   by Tana Hoban
Sorting by David Kirkby

Mary J. Murray, Mazomanie, WI

Butterfly Bonanza

LEARNING OBJECTIVES

The children will:

1. Identify colors.
2. Count objects.
3. Compare sizes and groups of objects.

Materials

colored tissue paper
scissors (adult only)
paper plate
3' x 3' white mural
    paper
plastic tub

VOCABULARY

big	color	fly
butterfly	count	small

PREPARATION

- Cut a large number of both 2" and 4" squares from colored tissue paper.
- Twist each square in the center, creating a butterfly shape.
- Gently place all the "butterflies" in a large plastic tub.

WHAT TO DO

1. Gather the children together on the floor in a large circle.
2. Use a paper plate to scoop a collection of butterflies from the tub and toss them over the heads of the children.
3. Invite each child to "catch" one butterfly.
4. Display the mural white paper in the center of the circle. Invite each child to describe her butterfly and then place it on the paper.
5. Drop several more scoops of butterflies onto the paper as the children watch them fly and land on the paper.
6. Gently pick up the paper and roll it into a cone shape (with the butterflies inside).
7. Unroll the paper and let the butterflies again "fly" over the heads of the children.
8. Repeat the activity, this time inviting children to collect several butterflies.

ASSESSMENT

To assess the children's learning, consider the following:

- Provide a child with 10 (or 20) images of butterflies. Can the child describe the color, sizes, and number of butterflies?

Mary J. Murray, Mazomanie, WI

Children's Books

From Caterpillar to Butterfly by Deborah Heiligman
Good Night, Sweet Butterflies by Dawn Bentley, Melanie Gerth, and Heather Cahoon
The Very Hungry Caterpillar by Eric Carle

Color Basket

3+

LEARNING OBJECTIVES

The children will:
1. Identify colors by name.
2. Identify shapes, letters, and numbers by name.

Materials

small basket with a
 handle
construction paper
 "cards" in assorted
 colors
space to play game

VOCABULARY

basket   cards   color names   find

PREPARATION

- Cut enough cards for each child to have a color (you may need to have more than one or two of each color).

WHAT TO DO

1. Seat all but one child on the floor in a circle.
2. Give the remaining child a basket, and give each seated child a card.
3. Ask the child with the basket to walk around the circle singing, "A tisket, a tasket, I have a color basket. Find the color ____, and put it in the basket!"
4. When she finds a child with that color card, she puts the card into the basket, then switches places with that child, and the game repeats.
5. Try the game again with shape, letter, number, or picture cards.

TEACHER-TO-TEACHER TIP

- Laminate the cards!

ASSESSMENT

To assess the children's learning, consider the following:
- As you collect the cards, hold each one up and ask the children to identify the color.

Children's Books

Colors Everywhere by
 Tana Hoban
I Love Colors! by
 Hans Wilhelm
Red, Blue, Yellow Shoe
 by Tana Hoban
*White Rabbit's Color
 Book* by Alan Baker

Carla LeMasters, Bartonville, IL

Color Card Game

LEARNING OBJECTIVES

The children will:

1. Identify colors.
2. Match like colors.
3. Follow directions.

Materials

two matching sets of colored shape card one colored shape per card

VOCABULARY

card   color names   quiet   shape

PREPARATION

● To make a set of colored shape cards, simply cut four different 4" shapes (circle, triangle, square, and rectangle) from red, yellow, green, blue, and orange paper.
● Glue each shape to a 5" x 7" note card. Make two sets of cards.

WHAT TO DO

1. Stack one deck of cards face down on the floor.
2. Hand out the other set of cards to the children, one card per child.
3. Tell the children that you will display a card from your deck and whoever has the matching card puts it face up next to your card.
4. Begin the game by turning over the first card. Wait for the child with the matching card to place her card next to yours. Continue until the children match all the cards.
5. Shuffle and deal the cards and hand them out again for another round of color shape fun. It is also fun to try playing this game without anyone speaking!

TEACHER-TO-TEACHER TIP

● Laminate the cards for durability.

ASSESSMENT

To assess the children's learning, consider the following:

● Use the note cards from the activity like a set of flash cards. Display each card as you invite children to identify the color of the shape on the card. Can each child identify the colors and shapes of all the cards?
● As an additional assessment, give one child a puppet, and then display several cards from the deck. Invite the child to have the puppet "talk" about the colors and shapes that are on display.

Children's Books

Color Zoo by Lois Ehlert
Shapes, Shapes, Shapes by Tana Hoban

Mary J. Murray, Mazomanie, WI

Colorful Caterpillars

3+

LEARNING OBJECTIVES

The children will:
1. Increase color recognition skills.
2. Improve small motor skills.
3. Practice counting.
4. Improve oral language skills.

Materials

30 or more colorful
  chenille stems
four large green felt
  leaves
one or more plastic
  bug catchers

VOCABULARY

caterpillar	crawl	leaf
color	fuzzy	small

PREPARATION

● Wrap a chenille stem around a marker to create a tight coil. Remove the marker for a fat caterpillar manipulative. Wrap the chenille stem around a pen for a skinny caterpillar manipulative. Make 30 or more colorful caterpillars.
● Place the caterpillars and leaves in the plastic bug catchers.

WHAT TO DO

1. Invite a child to open the bug catcher and remove a leaf.
2. The child spills out the caterpillars, places each caterpillar on the large felt leaf, and identifies the color of each caterpillar.
3. Encourage the children to sort the caterpillars by color or line them up in a row and count them.
4. Invite the children to move the caterpillars about the leaves as they work and play.

SONG

Invite the children to manipulate a caterpillar as they sing "Colorful Caterpillar."

Colorful Caterpillar by Mary J. Murray
(Tune: "Twinkle, Twinkle, Little Star")
Colorful caterpillar I like you.
Soft and fuzzy, friendly too.
Crawl upon a leaf.
Crawl all around.

Crawl up a tree. And then crawl down.
Colorful caterpillar I like you.
Soft and fuzzy, friendly too.

ASSESSMENT

To assess the children's learning, consider the following:
● Can each child name the colors of all the caterpillars in the bug catcher? (Display a caterpillar on a leaf and ask the child to name the color.)

Children's Books

Butterfly Express by Jane Belk Moncure
The Very Hungry Caterpillar by Eric Carle

Mary J. Murray, Mazomanie, WI

Find Your Favorite Color

3+

LEARNING OBJECTIVES

The children will:

1. Identify their favorite color.
2. Cooperate with a partner and interact with each other.

Materials

box or special bag
timer

VOCABULARY

box	favorite	minute	search
color	hunt	partner	time

WHAT TO DO

1. Ask the children to find a partner and give each pair a box or bag.
2. Ask the children to find as many items of their favorite color that they can fit inside the box or bag in a limited amount of time.
3. Put the timer on and tell the children to start searching. Give extra time to younger children who may get frustrated when the timer goes off.
4. Another option is to concentrate on a certain color for each pair or one color for the whole class. Do what works; also ask for suggestions from the children.

TEACHER-TO-TEACHER TIPS

- Allow children to work alone if they wish.
- You might also want to let each child take home one favorite item. For example, if Sophie likes red, put out a red pencil or other item for her to have.

POEM

Favorite Colors by Eileen Lucas
My favorite colors are pink and blue
And yours are white and red.
My mom prefers brown and yellow.
My dad likes purple and black.
Some days I really like them all
But that doesn't seem fair.
But then again there are so many colors
I don't think anyone would care.

Children's Books

All About Colors by
Ruth Thomson
A Color of His Own by
Leo Lionni
Mouse Paint by Ellen
Stoll Walsh

ASSESSMENT

To assess the children's learning, consider the following:

- Can each child identify her favorite color?
- Can each child identify other colors around the room as she plays the game?

Eileen Lucas, Fort McMurray, Alberta, Canada

I Can Sing a Rainbow

3+

LEARNING OBJECTIVES

The children will:

1. Identify the colors of the rainbow (red, orange, yellow, green, blue, indigo, violet).
2. Sequence themselves moving from one color to another color.

Materials

construction paper
scissors (adult only)
laminator
tape
CD player
CD including the song "I Can Sing a Rainbow" (if available)

VOCABULARY

cooperation   prism   rainbow   violet
indigo

PREPARATION

- Cut out a large number of paper squares (the colors of the rainbow) and laminate them. Each square should be large enough for at least one child to stand on.

WHAT TO DO

1. Put each color square on the floor, connecting them together to form one large square or rectangle.
2. Have the children form a circle around the big square or squares. Sing or play the song "I Can Sing a Rainbow" or any other song.
3. When the music or singing stops, call out a color of the rainbow.
4. The children run to that color and stand on it. There are several of the same color, so it should not be crowded; however, squares can and should be shared.
5. Sing or play the music again. When you stop singing or playing, call out another color and the children find and stand on this one. Timing can get faster as children learn the colors and feel comfortable moving in the space.

TEACHER-TO-TEACHER TIP

- Make sure that quiet or less active children get a chance to get to the rainbow square they want so they feel a sense of accomplishment and participation.

ASSESSMENT

To assess the children's learning, consider the following:

- Watch each child as she goes to the squares. Can she identify the colors on each square? Note which colors children have difficulty identifying.

Children's Books

Planting a Rainbow by Lois Ehlert
A Rainbow of My Own by Don Freeman

Annette Rivlin-Gutman Seattle, WA

It's a Match

LEARNING OBJECTIVES

The children will:

1. Learn how to recognize colors.
2. Develop their color matching skills.

Materials

object that matches the color of your shirt

VOCABULARY

different   match   same

WHAT TO DO

1. Ask the children to sit in a circle.
2. Once you have their attention, call out the color of your shirt.
3. Then, show the children an object that matches your shirt.
4. Reinforce the idea by asking the children to point out other objects in the room that match the color of your shirt.
5. Explain that you want all the children to find an object in the classroom that matches the shirts that they are wearing. (If any of the children are wearing striped or patterned shirts, assign them a single color from their shirts.)
6. Regroup and ask each child to take a turn showing the group her color match.

ASSESSMENT

To assess the children's learning, consider the following:

- Repeat the activity, asking the children to find objects that match their pants.
- Can the children think of ways that they match one other (such as wearing same color clothes, having similar hair, ages, and so on)? Suggest a few possibilities if they need help getting started.

Erin Huffstetler, Maryville, TN

Children's Books

A Color of His Own by Leo Lionni
A Pair of Socks by Stuart J. Murphy
Apples and Oranges: Going Bananas with Pairs by Sara Pinto

Rainbow Soup

3+

LEARNING OBJECTIVES

The children will:

1. Practice color recognition.
2. Develop their color matching skills.
3. Hone their listening skills.

Materials

large pot
large spoon
hat
color flash cards

VOCABULARY

different	match	recipe
ingredients	rainbow	same

PREPARATION

- If you do not have color flash cards, create a set out of colored construction paper. You will need one card for each child.

WHAT TO DO

1. Ask the children to sit in a circle. Place a pot in the middle and announce that you are going to make rainbow soup.
2. Place the necessary color ingredients (the color flash cards) into a hat, and have each child draw one.
3. Tell the children that you want them to find objects in the room that match the color of the card that they have chosen.
4. Call the children back to the circle once everyone has had time to find an object.
5. Ask each child to take a turn showing the "ingredient" that she has found. For each one, ask the children if the color of the "ingredient" matches the child's color card. If everyone agrees that it is a match, let the child add it to the pot and give the soup a few stirs.
6. After the children add all of the "ingredients," peek into the pot and announce that they have made rainbow soup. Yum!

ASSESSMENT

To assess the children's learning, consider the following:

- Ask the children to name their favorite foods and then name the color of each one.
- Ask each child to name her favorite color. Then ask each child to draw a picture of an object that is that color.

Children's Books

Planting a Rainbow by
Lois Ehlert
Stone Soup by
Marcia Brown

Erin Huffstetler, Maryville, TN

Sock Walk

3+

LEARNING OBJECTIVES

The children will:

1. Identify colors.
2. Match like colors.
3. Follow directions.
4. Improve large motor skills.

Materials

several pairs of
women's colored
socks, in a variety of
colors, one pair per
child

VOCABULARY

| arms | link | sock | walk |

WHAT TO DO

1. Have the children take off both of their shoes.
2. If the children are already wearing colored socks, have them display their feet and say the color of their socks.
3. For the remaining children, hand each child a pair of socks to put on over their own.
4. Invite the children to stand up and form a very large circle. (Use a gym or other large space, if possible.)
5. Have the children walk counterclockwise and single file around the circle.
6. Call out two colors, such as red and blue. The children wearing red and blue socks link arms together in groups of two or three and continue walking around the circle together. The rest of the children continue walking alone.
7. Continue the activity as various groups of children link arms and walk together as directed.
8. At any time, call out the word "rainbow." At that time, children join to form one long line by placing their hands on the shoulders or waist of the person in front of them, and walk in unison until you call the next two colors.
9. Play for several minutes.

ASSESSMENT

To assess the children's learning, consider the following:

- Have the children line up on one wall of the room. Call out a color and instruct children wearing the designated color of socks to walk to the other wall. Continue until all children have crossed the room.
- Place the socks in a laundry basket. Can the children work in pairs to match socks that are the same color?

Children's Books

Mouse Paint by
Ellen Stoll Walsh
A Pair of Socks by
Stuart J. Murphy

Mary J. Murray, Mazomanie, WI

Color Game

4

LEARNING OBJECTIVES

The children will:
1. Apply knowledge to a new context.
2. Respond to questions from other children.
3. Develop their large motor skills.

Materials

beanbag

VOCABULARY

aquamarine   tan   turquoise   violet

WHAT TO DO

1. Have all children stand in a circle. Ask one volunteer to start the game; give her the beanbag.
2. The child with the beanbag throws it to a child of her choice and calls out a color.
3. The child who catches the beanbag calls out an object that is the same color.
4. The child who caught the beanbag now gets a turn throwing.
5. Continue until every child has had a turn.
6. If you "run out" of colors, repeat colors but challenge the children to think of new objects.

ASSESSMENT

To assess the children's learning, consider the following:
- How well are the children matching the colors of objects to the correct color names?
- Are the children responding well to questions from peers in this large-group situation?

Freya Zellerhoff, Towson, MD

Children's Books

City Colors by Zoran Milich
Color by Ella Doran
I Spy Colors in Art by Lucy Micklethwait
Kid Tea by Elizabeth Ficocelli
My Many Colored Days by Dr. Seuss
Yellow Elephant: A Bright Bestiary by Julie Larios

Make It Whisper! A Marker Game

Materials

one set of eight colored water-based markers with lids

two white sheets of poster board approximately 16" x 20"

CD or cassette of upbeat music

LEARNING OBJECTIVES

The children will:

1. Learn how to cap a marker tightly so it does not dry out.
2. Follow directions.
3. Identify colors.

VOCABULARY

cap	color	marker	whisper
click	dry	tight	

WHAT TO DO

1. Ask the children to sit in a circle. Display two large sheets of poster board in the center of the circle.
2. Give a different colored marker to every other child in the circle. **Note:** Explain that it is important to put caps back on markers so they don't dry out.
3. Direct the children to pass the markers around the circle. After about 30 seconds, begin the music. When the music starts, whoever is holding a marker names its color and draws a simple design on one of the two pieces of chart paper in the center of the circle.
4. Stop the music and invite the children to make their marker "whisper." At that time everyone listens closely as the eight children "click" the cap tightly on their marker and then return to the circle.
5. Repeat the activity several times until everyone has had an opportunity to draw and "make a marker whisper."
6. Afterwards, display the posters of colorful art at the front of the classroom.

ASSESSMENT

To assess the children's learning, consider the following:

- Give one child a marker, and then put the marker caps on the floor in a row. Can the child name the colors of the marker caps? Can each child find the marker cap that matches her marker?
- Can the children write their names using different markers for each letter?

Mary J. Murray, Mazomanie, WI

Children's Books

City Colors by Zoran Milich

Colors by Dorling Kindersley

My Many Colored Days by Dr. Seuss

Secondary Color Match-Up 4+

Karyn F. Everham, Fort Myers, FL

LEARNING OBJECTIVES

The children will:
1. Differentiate between the colors green, purple, and orange.
2. Name the colors green, purple, and orange.
3. Learn how to follow directions.

Materials

18" lengths of orange, purple, and green silk or ribbon, one length per child
game board spinner with the same colors

VOCABULARY

| green | orange | ribbon | spinner |
| matching | purple | same | |

WHAT TO DO

1. Give each child one length of ribbon. Tell them the name of each color and ask them to repeat these names.
2. Spin the spinner and name the color it lands on. Then say, "If you are holding the matching color ____, wave your ribbon in the air."
3. Continue playing with different variations, such as, "Call out the color name three times," "Whisper the color name once," or "Wag your ribbon like a tail."
4. Let the children choose a different color, if desired.
5. Invite children who are comfortable leading the game to spin the spinner and name the color and instruction.

ASSESSMENT

To assess the children's learning, consider the following:
● Give the children sheets of orange, green, and purple paper. Can the children match the sheets of paper to like-colored items in the classroom, and name the colors of each item?

Children's Books

Green Wilma by Tedd Arnold
Harold and the Purple Crayon by Crockett Johnson

Songs

Sing or play recordings of "It's Not Easy Being Green" by Jim Henson or "The Green Grass Grows All Around" by Pete Seeger.

Carton o' Primary Colors

5+

LEARNING OBJECTIVES

The children will:
1. Differentiate between the colors red, blue, and yellow.
2. Match like colors in red, blue, and yellow.

Materials

half-dozen egg cartons, one per child
red, yellow, and blue crayon pieces, two per child

VOCABULARY

egg carton   match   same

PREPARATION

● In advance, mark the inside of each egg carton compartment with red, yellow, or blue.
● Place two red, two blue, and two yellow crayons inside each carton.

WHAT TO DO

1. Give each child a prepared egg carton.
2. Together count blue, red, and yellow crayons and egg holders.
3. Challenge the children to put the crayons in the matching sections of the carton.
4. Ask the children to close the containers (with the crayons inside) and shake the containers. Open again, and repeat the matching challenge.
5. Vary the challenge by having the children remove all but one crayon, and try to shake the crayon into the correct section.

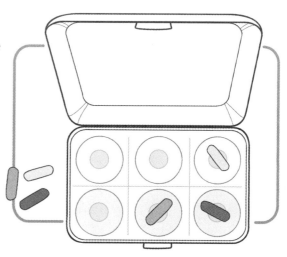

ASSESSMENT

To assess the children's learning, consider the following:
● Give the children pieces of red, yellow, and blue construction paper. Can the children separate the papers into three piles, sorting by color? Can they match the colored paper with items of like color found in the classroom?

Children's Books

Is It Red? Is It Yellow? Is It Blue? by Tana Hoban
Little Blue and Little Yellow by Leo Leonni
Marcos Colors: Red, Yellow, Blue by Tomie dePaola

Songs

Sing "Red, Red Robin" or "Yellow Submarine" with the children.

Karyn F. Everham, Fort Myers, FL

Color Bingo

5+

LEARNING OBJECTIVES

The children will:

1. Learn to recognize colors.
2. Follow verbal cues to find the colors under a letter.
3. Play an unusual version of Bingo.

Materials

white poster board cut
into 8" x 8" squares,
one per child

markers, paints,
colored pencils,
crayons, or brightly
colored pictures of
one color to use per
square

small Bingo markers
(pennies, round slips
of paper, erasers)

glue sticks

ruler

pencil

VOCABULARY

Bingo   combination   marker

PREPARATION

- Prepare BINGO cards by dividing them into sections like a BINGO card with five columns and four rows. Use a ruler to measure off spaces. Write C-O-L-O-R across the top.
- Pick 20 colors and color in the spaces under the letters. (Imagine the poster board as a BINGO card to get the idea.) Another variation is to put pictures that are mainly one color.
- Once the cards are completed, make a list of possible color-letter combinations and cut them into slips.

WHAT TO DO

1. Explain that Color BINGO is like regular BINGO.
2. Draw slips of color/letter combinations from a box and call them out ("'O' green," "'C' red").
3. Children place a marker over the square if they have the correct combination.
4. When a child has marked one color in each column, she shouts, "COLOR!"

ASSESSMENT

To assess the children's learning, consider the following:

- Can each child find the correct square to put her marker on when you call the combinations in the activity?

Donna Alice Patton, Hillsboro, OH

Children's Books

Batty for Black by
Christianne C. Jones
Brown at the Zoo by
Christianne C. Jones
Pink Takes a Bow by
Christianne C. Jones
Winter White by
Christianne C. Jones

What's My Color?

5+

LEARNING OBJECTIVES

The children will:
1. Learn teamwork skills as they practice simple grouping.
2. Identify colors and group using colors.

Materials

circles (7"–8") cut out
    of colored card
    stock (three or four
    different colors)
yarn
hole punch
large indoor space or
    outdoor play yard

VOCABULARY

necklace   teamwork   yarn

PREPARATION

● Punch a hole in each circle and run a length of yarn though. Tie yarn ends together to make "necklaces" children can wear.

WHAT TO DO

1. Give each child a "necklace." Pass out colors randomly.
2. Have the children sit down in a circle and talk with them about what teamwork means. Tell the children they are going to play a game using teamwork.
3. When the whistle blows, the children must stand up and start looking around at each other. They should look for other children who are wearing the same color circle, and stand by those children.
4. Encourage the children to talk to one another and help other children during this exercise. The game is done when all the children are standing in groups of matching colors.

TEACHER-TO-TEACHER TIP

● To make the activity easier at first, start with only two colors. As the children get better at working together, add more and more colors to increase the challenge.

ASSESSMENT

To assess the children's learning, consider the following:
● After playing the game a few times, have the children sit back down. Encourage them to talk about what they learned about working together. Is working together harder or easier then they thought? What other types of people work together?
● Talk about people like firefighters and construction workers. Can the children come up with their own examples of teamwork?

Children's Books

Barrels to the Moon by
    Harold Berson
A Color of His Own by
    Leo Lionni
Midnight Snowman by
    Caroline Feller Bauer
One Saturday Morning
    by Barbara Baker

Sarah Stasik, Roanoke, VA

Colorful Handprints

3+

LEARNING OBJECTIVES

The children will:

1. Identify colors.
2. Match colors.
3. Read color names.

Materials

colored construction
   paper
scissors (adult only)
tagboard
marker
pocket chart (optional)

VOCABULARY

color names   color wheel   primary color
              handprint   secondary color

PREPARATION

- Create two sets of cards. Cut out colored handprints for one set. Use tagboard to print the names of the colors on the other set.

WHAT TO DO

1. Set out the color nametags and colored handprints.
2. Have the children match the color names to the colored handprints.
3. As the children are matching the color names and handprints, engage them in a discussion about the colors names, and the order of colors on the color wheel.
4. Talk with the children about the qualities of the various colors (warm colors and cool colors, primary and secondary colors).
5. Challenge the children to put the matching handprints and color name cards together in a pocket chart in the order that matches the color wheel.

TEACHER-TO-TEACHER TIPS

- Use a pocket chart, if available.
- For a shortcut, use bulletin board trim with handprints to make handprint cards.
- For younger children, print the color names in the corresponding color.
- Laminate the cards for durability.

ASSESSMENT

To assess the children's learning, consider the following:

- Discuss with the children how they matched the color names to the handprints. Reread the color names with the children. Encourage the children's use of small motor skills by asking them to place cards in the pocket chart.

Jackie Wright, Enid, OK

Children's Books

Color Farm by
   Lois Ehlert
A Color of His Own by
   Leo Lionni
My Hands Can by
   Jean Holzenthaler

I Spy Colors in a Bottle

3+

LEARNING OBJECTIVES

The children will:
1. Sort objects by color.
2. Control small muscles while handling small objects.

Materials

clean, empty soda or
  water bottles (20
  ounces; one per
  child)
black permanent
  marker
small white pebbles
lots of different
  colored beads and
  trinkets, craft jewels,
  sequins, or other
  little "treasures" that
  fit in soda bottles
funnel
plastic spoon

VOCABULARY

color wheel   primary color   secondary color
colors of the
  rainbow

PREPARATION

● Remove labels from bottles and write "I spy…" on each bottle using a
  permanent marker.

WHAT TO DO

1. Explain to the children that are going to create a treasure bottle that contains
   three hidden colors. Ask each child to pick a handful of treasures in three
   different colors (such as green, purple, and red).
2. Write the name of the three colors on each child's bottle using a permanent
   marker. Older children can write the words themselves, with your help. (For
   example, "I spy green, purple, and red.")
3. Have the children use funnels to put the assorted treasures in their bottles and
   then pour pebbles or a similar material on top of their treasures until the
   bottles are half full. Close lids tightly.
4. The children shake their bottles. See if they can identify one or more objects of
   each color in their bottles.

ASSESSMENT

To assess the children's learning, consider the following:
● Discuss with the children how they sort by color. Observe their attention span
  and peer interaction. Are the children involved in the activity?
● Are the children exhibiting an age-appropriate level of small motor
  development?

Freya Zellerhoff, Towson, MD

Children's Books

*Brown Bear, Brown
Bear, What Do You See?*
by Bill Martin, Jr.
A Color of His Own by
Leo Lionni
*The Mixed-Up
Chameleon* by
Eric Carle
Planting a Rainbow by
Lois Ehlert

Matching Color Word Cards 4+

LEARNING OBJECTIVES

The children will:
1. Read the names of colors.
2. Match the color word to the correct color.

Materials

colored construction
    paper
markers
scissors (adult only)
white card stock

VOCABULARY

color names (red, orange, yellow, green, blue, purple)

PREPARATION

- Cut a set of color cards and white cards in the same dimensions.
- Write the name of a color on each of the white cards and laminate (write the word *yellow* with a yellow marker, *green* in green, and so on, or use a black marker to reduce the visual scaffolding).

WHAT TO DO

1. Pick up a color card and tell the children the color name.
2. Show the matching word card and have the children identify it. You can start simply by using only a few cards.
3. Encourage the children to play matching games on the floor, table, or white board. For example, line the color cards up on the white board and hand a child a word card. Help him read it, if necessary. Then ask him to place the word card under the corresponding color card.
4. For a language game, give each child a color card or a word card. Encourage children to seek out the child who has their color or word card match.

TEACHER-TO-TEACHER TIPS

- For an extra challenge, children can discuss the spelling of words like *silver*, *purple*, *light blue*, *brown*, and *white*.
- Also consider placing the word cards or color cards on the white board and having the children write the color names under the cards with a white board marker.

ASSESSMENT

To assess the children's learning, consider the following:
- Children are very interested in matching and writing tasks of all kinds, so these stimulating materials will address multiple developmental needs. Discuss the matching the children did and ask them how they found the matching items.

Children's Books

I Love Colors by Margaret Miller
My Crayons Talk by Patricia Hubbard

Patrick Mitchell, Yagoto, Nagoya, Japan

Button Count

3+

LEARNING OBJECTIVES

The children will:
1. Identify the color green.
2. Identify numbers.
3. Practice counting from 1–5.

Materials

green buttons
white construction
   paper
green marker

VOCABULARY

buttons   count   green   numbers

PREPARATION

● Using the green marker, draw lines on the construction paper to divide it into five sections. Number each section from 1–5. Draw the corresponding numbers of dots next to each number. For example, one dot next to 1, two dots next to 2, and so on.

WHAT TO DO

1. Set out the construction paper and green buttons. Ask the children to identify the color of the buttons.
2. Tell the children to place the indicated number of buttons in each section.
3. Once they have placed their buttons on their paper, count with them to check and see if they have the correct number in each section.
4. If appropriate, help the children identify the materials.

POEM

Green by Laura Wynkoop
Shamrocks and turtles
And evergreen trees,
Iguanas and pickles
And lettuce and peas.
Snakes and zucchini,
And ivy and ferns,
It's easy to see green
Wherever one turns.

| 1 | 2 | 3 | 4 | 5 |
| 1 | 2 | 3 | 4 | 5 |

Children's Books

Colors: Green by
   Esther Sarfatti
Green by
   Sarah L. Schuette
Green as a Bean by
   Karla Kuskin

ASSESSMENT

To assess the children's learning, consider the following:
● Review the color of the buttons and the numbers 1–5.
● Did the children place the correct number of buttons in each section of the construction paper?

Laura Wynkoop, San Dimas, CA

Cereal Mania

3+

LEARNING OBJECTIVES

The children will:

1. Learn how to sort colors.
2. Create different color patterns.
3. Fine tune their small motor skills.

Materials

colorful breakfast
  cereal rings
bags or cups
poster board
markers
chenille stems

VOCABULARY

order   pattern   sequence   sorting

PREPARATION

● Put a handful of cereal into bags or cups. Make one for each child.
● Draw color patterns on the poster board. Possible patterns include red, yellow, red, yellow; blue, green, orange, blue, green, orange; or green, yellow, blue, blue, green, yellow, blue, blue.

WHAT TO DO

1. Talk about patterns. Show the children the patterns on the poster board and ask them which color follows each sequence.
2. Give each child a bag or cup of cereal. Tell them not to eat it yet!
3. Explain to the children that they are going to copy the color patterns using their cereal. Have them sort each pile of cereal by color. For young children, use simple patterns, such as red, blue, red, blue.
4. Ask older children to copy the patterns on the poster board by arranging the cereal loops in the same patterns onto chenille stems. Demonstrate by making one yourself.
5. After the children create their patterns, invite them to eat their patterns!

TEACHER-TO-TEACHER TIPS

● For older children, have them create their own patterns.
● Also consider letting them string the cereal on yarn to make necklaces or bracelets.

ASSESSMENT

To assess the children's learning, consider the following:

● Walk around to observe the cereal patterns. If the children created their own patterns, ask them to share their favorite patterns with all the children.

Children's Books

Bread and Cereal by
Tea Benduhn
I Like Cereal by
Jennifer Julius
Sort It Out by
Barbara Mariconda

Angela Hawkins, Denver, CO

Color Cans

3+

LEARNING OBJECTIVES

The children will:
1. Learn color word recognition.
2. Sort various objects by colors.

eight empty coffee
  cans, one for each
  color
white construction
  paper
marker
die cuts in various
  colors
various objects of
  different colors
basket

VOCABULARY

black	green	purple	sorting
blue	orange	red	white
brown			

PREPARATION

● Cover coffee cans with white construction paper.
● Write the appropriate color names on the outside of each can and add various die cuts.

WHAT TO DO

1. In advance, introduce the skill of sorting and or classifying.
2. Collect various objects and manipulatives that are the same colors of the cans. Place all objects in a basket.
3. As children pick out objects, discuss what the object is and what color it is. Children then place that object in the appropriate can.

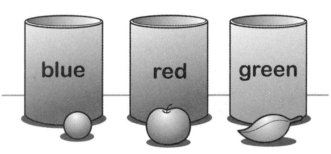

ASSESSMENT

To assess the children's learning, consider the following:
● Show the children several items of different colors. Can they name the items, name their colors, and sort the items by color?

Jason Verdone, Woodbury, NJ

Children's Books

Color Zoo by
  Lois Ehlert
My Many Colored Days
  by Dr. Seuss
*My Very First Book of
  Colors* by Eric Carle

Colorful Ribbon Cups

3+

LEARNING OBJECTIVES

The children will:
1. Identify colors.
2. Compare lengths.
3. Think analytically.

Materials

four large colorful
    ceramic coffee mugs
spools of colorful
    ribbon in six or
    more different colors
scissors (adult only)

VOCABULARY

color	long	ribbon
cup	measure	short

PREPARATION

- Cut strands of the colored ribbon into different lengths.
- Place one strand of each color in each cup. Each cup should contain six different colored strands of varying lengths.
- Display the cups at a table.

WHAT TO DO

1. Invite a small group of children to work at a table.
2. Have each child select a cup and talk about its colors.
3. Instruct the children to take turns removing one ribbon at a time from their cups.
4. As each child lifts a ribbon straight up and out of the cup, ask her to name the color and then comment on how long the ribbon is.
5. Ask each child to place each ribbon out on the table.
6. The children take turns removing colorful ribbons and comparing lengths of the ribbons in their own cups.
7. Afterwards, the children may compare lengths of their ribbons with one another.
8. When the children are finished, have the children place all the ribbons back in their original cups.

ASSESSMENT

To assess the children's learning, consider the following:
- Place pairs of ribbons on a table. Can each child name the colors of the ribbons and then say which ribbon is longer or shorter?
- Put the ribbons end to end on the carpet. Invite a child to drive a small toy car down the length of the ribbons and talk about the colors as she manipulates the car.

Children's Books

Red, Blue, Yellow Shoe
    by Tana Hoban
Ribbon Rescue by
    Robert Munsch

Mary J. Murray, Mazomanie, WI

Fishing for Colors

3+

LEARNING OBJECTIVES

The children will:
1. Match colors.
2. Count to 10.
3. Compare numbers using a bar graph.

Materials

large sheet of butcher
    or colored paper
colored markers
colored construction
    paper
paper clips
dowel rods or sticks
magnets
colored string

VOCABULARY

bar graph   fish   magnet   most

PREPARATION

- Cut fish shapes out of construction paper. Make 10 for each color used.
- Put a paper clip on the nose of each fish.
- Use dowel rods or sticks, string, and magnets to make fishing poles with magnets on the end. Make one rod for each color using corresponding string colors.
- Use markers to make a large bar graph outline on a large sheet of butcher or colored paper with a column for each color.

WHAT TO DO

1. Make a pond by putting all the fish cutouts in a circle on the floor.
2. Gather the children around the pond. Show them how the magnet on the fishing pole picks up the fish by the paper-clipped nose.
3. Split the group of children into teams for each color and have each team line up behind a team leader. Explain that they will have three minutes (adjust the time depending on the children's skills) to catch as many fish of their color as they can. As they catch a fish, they should place it on the bar graph.
4. Time the first fishing group. When they are done, have the children count how many fish they put on the graph. Compare the numbers and discuss correlation of most fish and tallest column.
5. Repeat until all children have a chance to fish.

ASSESSMENT

To assess the children's learning, consider the following:
- When asked to pick out colors that match their color, can the children successfully choose matching colors?

Jennifer Reilly, Grand Junction, CO

Children's Books

A Color of His Own by
    Leo Lionni
Giraffe Graphs by
    Melissa Stewart
Ten Little Fish by
    Audrey Wood

My Favorite Melon

3+

LEARNING OBJECTIVES

The children will:
1. Learn about healthy food.
2. Identify colors.
3. Practice writing their names.
4. Learn about voting.

Materials

watermelon
cantaloupe
honeydew
poster board or other
    large paper
sticky notes

VOCABULARY

melons (watermelon, cantaloupe,
    honeydew)

relations (greater, less)
vote

PREPARATION

- Cut the melons into cubes small enough for the children to eat.
- Divide the poster board into three sections. Color each section to match one of the melons: pink for watermelon, orange for cantaloupe, and green for honeydew. If desired, add a picture of each melon.

What is your favorite melon?

Kit	Greg	
Sam	Kellie	Jillian
Lily	Mike	Ben
watermelon	cantaloupe	honeydew

WHAT TO DO

1. Show the children the three melons (or pictures of the three melons).
2. Ask them to name the colors of the melons.
3. Discuss how the melons are the same and how they are different.
4. Provide each child with samples of all three melons. Have them taste the melons and decide which one they like best.
5. Have each child write her name on a sticky note and place it on the poster board in the section of the melon she likes best.
6. When all children have voted, discuss the results of the poll. Which melon received the greatest number of votes? Which melon received the least number of votes?

ASSESSMENT

To assess the children's learning, consider the following:
- Ask the children to identify the colors of the melons.
- Ask the children to practice writing their names again after the activity.

Children's Books

The Adventures of Melon and Turnip by Trisha Adelena Howell
Agrupemos Alimentos/Sorting Foods by Patricia Whitehaus
Planting a Rainbow by Lois Ehlert

Janet Hammond, Mount Laurel, NJ

What Color Will Your Doll Wear?

Materials

Brown Bear, Brown Bear, What Do You See? by Bill Martin, Jr.
My Very First Book of Colors by Eric Carle
paper dolls with paper clothes of different colors or real dolls with real clothes

LEARNING OBJECTIVES

The children will:
1. Listen to and discuss stories about colors.
2. Practice matching colors.
3. Become familiar with same and different using colors.

VOCABULARY

colors   doll   matching   same
different

WHAT TO DO

1. Read the books with the children.
2. Discuss the colors in the book and in the children's environment.
3. After reading the book, invite the children to play with the dolls.
4. Talk about the colors that are the same and colors that are different.
5. Invite them to dress the dolls with matching colors.

TEACHER-TO-TEACHER TIP

● If using paper dolls and clothes, let the children glue their dressed dolls onto a large piece of paper. Children may enjoy making entire families of dolls. If the paper is large enough, encourage the children to draw things the family likes to do together.

ASSESSMENT

To assess the children's learning, consider the following:
● Observe as the children play with the dolls and clothes. Ask questions such as, "What color are you putting on your doll?" "Are the colors on this doll the same or different?" and so on.
● During transition times, ask the children, "Do your clothes have any colors that match the clothes of other children in the class?"

Eileen Lucas, Fort McMurray, Alberta, Canada

Children's Books

Color Zoo by Lois Ehlert
Polar Bear, Polar Bear, What Do You Hear? by Bill Martin, Jr.

Following Directions

5+

LEARNING OBJECTIVES

The children will:

1. Draw different shapes (circle, triangle, square, and rectangle).
2. Practice color recognition and number recognition (1–4).

Materials

paper and crayons for each child

VOCABULARY

color names   crayon   paper   shape names

WHAT TO DO

1. Bring the children over to the table.
2. If desired, review shapes, numbers, and colors with the children. After reviewing, hand out the paper and crayons.
3. Explain to the children they will be doing an activity using shapes, numbers, and colors. They will need to listen carefully and follow the directions. Then ask them to do one or more of the following:
   - Draw a red square.
   - Draw a green rectangle.
   - Draw a yellow triangle.
   - Draw a blue circle.

   When you are finished with the shapes, ask them to do the following:
   - Draw a black 1.
   - Draw a brown 2.
   - Draw an orange 3.
   - Draw a purple 4.
4. When they are finished, gather the papers and review them with the group.

ASSESSMENT

To assess the children's learning, consider the following:

- Discuss whether all the papers are the same, and ask children if it was difficult to follow the directions.
- Review the shapes, colors, and numbers you worked with during the activity. If children had difficulty with any of these areas, plan activities to help the children further develop these skills.

Sherri Lawrence, Louisville, KY

Children's Books

Shapes by Jane Horne
Shapes, Shapes, Shapes by Tana Hoban
When a Line Bends, a Shape Begins by Rhonda Gowler Greene

Graph Us

5+

LEARNING OBJECTIVES

The children will:
1. Collect data to create a bar graph.
2. Draw a bar graph.
3. Read a bar graph.

Materials

dry-erase board
dry-erase markers
poster board
markers or crayons

VOCABULARY

bar   graph   information   organized

PREPARATION

● Draw the grid for a bar graph on the dry-erase board and the poster board.

WHAT TO DO

1. Explain to the children that a graph is a way to organize information. It makes information easier to see and understand, making it easier to answer questions about the information. Tell them they are going to make a graph of shirt colors.
2. Talk with the children about what colors they are wearing.
3. Count how many children are wearing a color. Make a bar on the dry-erase board. For example, if two people are wearing red shirts, draw one square for each shirt so that the bar is two squares tall. If appropriate, ask a child to draw a similar bar on the poster board.
4. Repeat with each color, asking children to take turns coloring the bars on the poster board.
5. Once the information is organized on this graph, discuss it with the children. What color are the most people wearing? The fewest? Are the same number of people wearing two colors? How can you tell? Which colors are they?
6. Discuss with the children what else they could graph.

TEACHER-TO-TEACHER TIP

● If several people are wearing patterned shirts, create a bar for "pattern" or "many colors."

Children's Books

Giraffe Graphs by Melissa Stuart
Graphs by Bonnie Bader
Tiger Math by Ann Whitehead Nagda

ASSESSMENT

To assess the children's learning, consider the following:
● Did the children participate in collecting the data?
● Did each child mark the poster board?
● Engage the children in answering questions about the bar graph. Do they exhibit an understanding of its information?

Sue Bradford Edwards, Florissant, MO

Good Morning, Color

3+

LEARNING OBJECTIVES

The children will:
1. Develop social skills.
2. Recognize colors.
3. Improve oral language skills.

Materials

eight beanbag pals or stuffed animals of different colors

eight objects of different colors to match each animal color

eight paper towels

VOCABULARY

colors   good morning   goodnight   uncover

cover

PREPARATION

- Display the animals in a row at the front of the classroom.
- Display an object of the same color in each animal's lap or hands.
- Cover each animal with a paper towel, up to its neck like a blanket, as if each animal is sleeping. The object in each animal's lap should be hidden by the paper towel.

WHAT TO DO

1. Tell the children that each animal's name is the same as its color. For example, "The blue whale's name is Blue. The red monkey's name is Red," and so on.
2. Remove the "blanket" from the first animal in line, as the children say, "Good morning, Blue."
3. Tell the children what Blue is holding (a blue car).
4. Uncover the next animal as children say, "Good morning, Red." Tell the children what the animal is holding.
5. Continue the activity until all eight animals have been greeted.
6. At the end of the day, repeat the activity, saying "goodnight" to each animal as you cover them back up.
7. Each morning, place a new matching-color object in the lap of each animal.

ASSESSMENT

To assess the children's learning, consider the following:
- Pet each animal individually as the children say the color and name of each animal. Ask the children questions such as, "What is Blue holding?" "What is Yellow holding?" Invite children to describe the object and its color.

Mary J. Murray, Mazomanie, WI

Children's Books

Freight Train by Donald Crews

Harold and the Purple Crayon by Crockett Johnson

Planting a Rainbow by Lois Ehlert

Color Hokey Pokey

3+

LEARNING OBJECTIVES

The children will:

1. Recognize colors.
2. Name colors.
3. Coordinate movement with color recognition.

Materials

red, yellow, blue, and green paper (one of each for each child)

VOCABULARY

circle   color names   rainbow

WHAT TO DO

1. Ask the children to form a circle. Hand each a set of colored papers. Begin with two or three colors
2. Sing "The Hokey Pokey," substituting the phrase "Put your red card in…" for the body parts. Go slowly so the children have time to shuffle their papers as needed.
3. Let the children take turns choosing the selected colors.
4. End with either "Put all the colors in…."
5. When the children become more skilled, increase the number of colors you give to each child.
6. For extra fun, include a rainbow-colored piece of paper and end with "Put the rainbow in…."

TEACHER-TO-TEACHER TIP

● If your children struggle with certain colors, emphasize those in the game. Children can play this game with any kind of item from shapes to letters.

ASSESSMENT

To assess the children's learning, consider the following:

● Review the names of the colors they are holding. Can the children follow directions while you sing them?

Children's Books

Hokey Pokey: Another Prickly Love Story by Lisa Wheeler
I Love Colors by Margaret Miller

Jaclyn Miller, Mishawaka, IN

Color Song

3+

LEARNING OBJECTIVES

The children will:

1. Respond to the directions in the song.
2. Review and reinforce their recognition of colors.
3. Learn a new song.

Materials

poster board
markers
card stock or colored
    construction paper
scissors (adult only)
tape

VOCABULARY

circle   color names

PREPARATION

● Prepare a song chart with words to the song printed with appropriate blanks.
● Make cards with color names written on them or circles of assorted colors to place in the blanks.

WHAT TO DO

1. Invite the children to sit in a group and to use "their listening ears."
2. Sing the following song with the children:

   Color Song by Margery Kranyik Fermino
   (Tune: "Mary Had a Little Lamb")
   If you're wearing something red, something red, something red,
   If you're wearing something red, stand and wave to us.

3. Repeat the song using other colors while placing the colored circles or color names in the song chart.
4. Invite children to choose a color for everyone to sing and place the appropriate symbol on the chart.

TEACHER-TO-TEACHER TIP

● It is easy to use this song for transitions by singing, "Go and stand in line" or "Go and get your snack" instead of "Stand and wave to us."

ASSESSMENT

To assess the children's learning, consider the following:

● Can the children connect the color names in the song to corresponding articles of clothing?
● Review the concept of following directions by asking the children what part of the song is a direction.

Children's Books

Brown Bear, Brown Bear, What Do You See? by Bill Martin, Jr.
My Very First Book of Colors by Eric Carle
Oso pardo, oso pardo, que ves ahi? by Bill Martin, Jr.
Red Is a Dragon by Roseanne Thong

Margery Kranyik Fermino, West Roxbury, MA

Colorful Xylophone

3+

LEARNING OBJECTIVES

The children will:
1. Sing musical notes.
2. Keep a beat.
3. Learn about color.

Materials

xylophone and mallet
color chart

VOCABULARY

| music | note | sing | xylophone |

WHAT TO DO

1. Gather the children around the xylophone.
2. Select a color from the color chart, then play two notes on the xylophone. Play a continuous rhythm alternating between the two notes.
3. Then sing the color according to the two notes. For example if you play E and C consecutively sing the words "blue blue" as you alternate playing E and C.
4. Invite the children to sing the tune for "blue" along with you.
5. Tap the highest note on the xylophone signaling children to stop and listen.
6. Select a different color and two different notes on the xylophone.
7. Repeat the activity several times, incorporating various simple melodies as you sing the colors of the rainbow.

TEACHER-TO-TEACHER TIP

● Use a piano or simple percussion instruments if you do not have a xylophone.

ASSESSMENT

To assess the children's learning, consider the following:
● Have the children form a line in front of the xylophone. Listen as each individual child sings the color melody on her own.
● Allow the children to try the activity on their own. Have a child play a two-note melody and sing a color word, as you repeat the melody to them.
● If you are using a toy xylophone with colorful keys, invite the children to sing each color as you move up and down the scale, according to the color of the keys on the xylophone.

Children's Books

I Love Colors by
Margaret Miller
*My Very First Book of
Colors* by Eric Carle
Red by
Karen Bryant-Mole
Red Is a Dragon by
Roseanne Thong

Mary J. Murray, Mazomanie, WI

Moving Colors

3+

LEARNING OBJECTIVES

The children will:
1. Review and reinforce their knowledge of colors.
2. Follow the directions in the song.
3. Develop large motor coordination.

Materials

6" circles or shape of your choice in assorted colors (one for each child)

VOCABULARY

above	hop	skip
below	jump	turn

PREPARATION

● Prepare classroom space for children to have enough room to stand and move.

WHAT TO DO

1. Distribute one circle to each child.
2. Invite children to "tune in" to listen and follow the directions to the following song:

Moving Colors by Margery Kranyik Fermino
(Tune: "Mary Had a Little Lamb")
If you have a red circle, red circle, red circle,
If you have a red circle, please jump up and down.

Everybody wave your shape, wave your shape, wave your shape,
Everybody wave your shape and slowly sit right down.

(Additional verses)
If you have a blue circle…move it side to side.
If you have a yellow circle…hold it way up high.
If you have an orange circle…move it up and down.
If you have a green circle…move it way down low.
If you have a purple circle…march right in your place.
If you have a brown circle…turn around and 'round.

Children's Books

Colors and shapes/Los Colores y las figuras by Gladys Rosa-Mendoza
The Many Colored Days by Dr. Seuss

ASSESSMENT

To assess the children's learning, consider the following:
● Are the children able to follow the directions in the song and recognize the colors?
● Did everyone participate in the activity?

Margery Kranyik Fermino, West Roxbury, MA

Musical Colors

3+

LEARNING OBJECTIVES

The children will:

1. Identify colors.
2. Increase listening skills.
3. Develop large motor skills.

Materials

construction paper
squares in red,
yellow, orange,
green, blue, and
purple
masking tape
stereo
CD or tape of upbeat
music

VOCABULARY

blue	orange	red
green	purple	yellow

PREPARATION

- Tape the squares on the floor around the classroom. There should be one square for every child in the class. Place a CD or tape in the stereo.

WHAT TO DO

1. Point out different squares on the classroom floor and help the children identify the colors.
2. Ask every child to stand on a square.

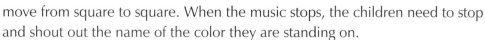

3. Play the music and have the children move from square to square. When the music stops, the children need to stop and shout out the name of the color they are standing on.
4. Vary the movements by having the children walk from square to square, or hop, skip, tiptoe, dance, and so on.

ASSESSMENT

To assess the children's learning, consider the following:

- Review the color names with the children as well as what they did during the activity when the music stopped and started.

Laura Wynkoop, San Dimas, CA

Children's Books

Color Dance by
Ann Jonas
Mouse Paint by Ellen
Stoll Walsh
*White Rabbit's Color
Book* by Alan Baker

T-Shirt Dance

3+

LEARNING OBJECTIVES

The children will:
1. Move their bodies to music.
2. Identify colors.
3. Develop large motor skills.

Materials

masking tape
bright-colored T-shirts,
    women's size small
    or medium
music

VOCABULARY

color	move	T-shirt
dance	music	

PREPARATION

● Place two lengths of masking tape about 20' long and 5' apart down the center of the gymnasium or another open area.

WHAT TO DO

1. Provide the children with colored T-shirts to put on over their clothes.
2. Have the children sit in two lines on the masking tape, facing each other.
3. Suggest that the children roll a beach ball back and forth across to one another. As each child receives the ball, invite her to name the color of her own T-shirt.
4. Invite the children to find their own place to move around in the gym, as you begin the music.
5. Ask the children to dance and move to the music, showing off their colors.
6. After several minutes, toss the beach ball up into the air and turn off the music, signaling children to stop moving.
7. Encourage the children to exchange T-shirts with a classmate and then return to the two masking tape lines.
8. Repeat the beach ball rolling activity and begin the music again.
9. Continue until the children have been able to "dance" in several different colors.

TEACHER-TO-TEACHER TIP

● Purchase bright-colored T-shirts at rummage sales or resale shops. After washing them, keep them at school for a variety of color activities.

ASSESSMENT

To assess the children's learning, consider the following:
● Listen as the children identify the colors of the T-shirts they are wearing. After the activity, invite children to stand on the lines and bat the beach ball back and forth as children name the colors of their pants, their own shirt, their socks, and so on.

Children's Books

Color Dance by
    Ann Jonas
Mouse Paint by Ellen
    Stoll Walsh
A Pair of Socks by
    Stuart J. Murphy

Mary J. Murray, Mazomanie, WI

Rhythmic Gymnastics

4+

LEARNING OBJECTIVES

The children will:

1. Learn about different colors.
2. Learn about different shapes.

new, unsharpened
    pencils (one for each
    child)
CD
stereo
lace ribbons of
    different colors
glue or thread

VOCABULARY

circle   snake   spiral   twirl

PREPARATION

● Cut ribbon into strips about 3' long and attach them to the pencils with glue or thread. Make one for each child.

WHAT TO DO

1. Talk to the children about rhythmic gymnastics and divide them into groups (one for each color).
2. Name each group according to the colors—red, blue, green, purple. Children should be at least 6' away from each other to avoid tangling ribbons.
3. Play the music and let the children twirl their ribbon pencils in the air and create new patterns (circle, spiral, snake, and so on).
4. Encourage the children to exchange the sticks and continue dancing.

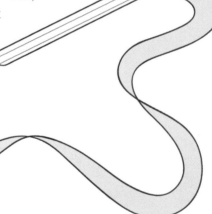

ASSESSMENT

To assess the children's learning, consider the following:

● Can the children name the colors of the pieces of ribbon?
● Name a color and ask the children whose ribbon is that color to come forward and twirl their ribbon pencils.

Shyamala Shanmugasundaram, Nerul, Navi Mumbai, India

Children's Books

Color Dance by
Ann Jonas
Pip and Kip by
Gina Erickson

Color Dash

3+

LEARNING OBJECTIVES

The children will:

1. Identify colors.
2. Follow simple rules.
3. Practice large motor skills.
4. Work in teams.

Materials

colored balls (ball pit
  balls work well)
box, bin, or pail to
  store each color ball

VOCABULARY

ball   relay   run   team

PREPARATION

- Make sure there are an equal number of balls in each color to be collected. Spread the balls out in a large open area. The balls should be spread out and not grouped by color. Set up the collection bins where the teams will line up.

WHAT TO DO

1. Divide the children into teams. There should be the same number of teams as there are number of colors.
2. Assign each team a color. Each team's color represents the color of balls the team will collect.
3. Have each team form a line near their collection bin.
4. Each team will work as a relay. The first child runs to find a ball matching the team color, returns, and puts the ball in the bin.
5. The next child then runs to find another ball matching the team color, returns, and puts the ball in the bin.
6. The relay continues until all of the team's balls have been found and placed in the bin.

TEACHER-TO-TEACHER TIP

- This activity also works well with plastic eggs as a springtime activity.

ASSESSMENT

To assess the children's learning, consider the following:

- Were the children able to work together in teams?
- Did the children collect only balls that matched their team colors?

Janet Hammond, Mount Laurel, NJ

Children's Books

My Colors by
Rebecca Emberley
*Nature's Paintbrush:
The Patterns and Colors
Around You* by
Susan Stockdale

Fly Away, Colors!

3+

LEARNING OBJECTIVES

The children will:

1. Learn to recognize colors.
2. Learn to match colors.

Materials

folded strips of
  construction paper
  in red, yellow,
  orange, green, blue,
  purple
stapler (adult only)
crepe paper strips in
  red, yellow, orange,
  green, blue, purple
two sets of crayons

VOCABULARY

color names   rhyme

PREPARATION

● Cut construction paper into 3" x 9" strips, folded to make 1½" x 9" in red, yellow, orange, green, blue, and purple.
● Staple three 24" strips of matching crepe paper on each band of folded paper.

WHAT TO DO

1. Ask each child to choose his favorite color band. Loosely staple the bands around the children's wrists.
2. Outside, designate two separate areas and divide the children into two groups.
3. Ask one group to choose a color and chant the following rhyme:

Color Bands by Susan Oldham Hill
Red band, red band, fly away.   *Red band, red band, now we say:*
Red band, red band, come and play.   *Red band, red band, stay all day!*

4. When the chant is finished, all the red bands from the other group "fly" to the second area.
5. Ask the other group to choose a color and chant the rhyme calling that color.

TEACHER-TO-TEACHER TIP

● Suggest colors for the groups to chant to make sure everyone has a chance to "fly" to the other group.

ASSESSMENT

To assess the children's learning, consider the following:

● Ask the children, one by one, to name the colors of one set of three or four crayons.
● Set out a second set of crayons. Can the children match the colors of the two sets?

Children's Books

Color Dance by
Ann Jonas
Colors Everywhere by
Tana Hoban
Of Colors and Things by
Tana Hoban
*What Makes a
Rainbow?* by Betty Ann
Schwartz

Susan Oldham Hill, Lakeland, FL

Rainbow Run

3+

LEARNING OBJECTIVES

The children will:

1. Identify colors.
2. Listen for directions.
3. Improve their large motor skills.

Materials

2' segments of crepe paper streamers in different colors (or strips of colored fabric)

VOCABULARY

blow	move	streamer
flag	run	wind

WHAT TO DO

1. Invite the children to line up on one side of the playground.
2. Hand each child a colored streamer.
3. Stand on the opposite side of the playground and call out, "Red run over."
4. Children holding the red streamers raise their streamers high in the air and run to the other side of the playground.
5. Repeat the command using a different color name.
6. Children will enjoy running with the streamers blowing in the wind as they move across the playground.
7. Continue until every color group has come across. Repeat the activity several times, allowing children to exchange colors with classmates for each round of the game.

SONG

See Our Colors Fly by Mary J. Murray
(Tune: "Here We Go 'Round the Mulberry Bush")
This is the way we run across, run across, run across.
This is the way we run across to see our colors fly.

ASSESSMENT

To assess the children's learning, consider the following:

- Observe the children to see if they recognize their color when you call it.
- Display an assortment of crepe paper streamers. Ask one child to pick up a specific color and wave it in the air.
- Place the streamers end to end. Invite the children to walk along the length of streamers and name each color as they pass by.

Children's Books

Red, Blue, Yellow Shoe by Tana Hoban
Why Is the Sky Blue? by Chris Arvetis

Mary J. Murray, Mazomanie, WI

Spot That Shirt!

3+

LEARNING OBJECTIVES

The children will:
1. Exercise large motor skills.
2. Practice identifying colors.
3. Practice following instructions.

Materials

colorful shirts, sashes, or arm bands
whistle

VOCABULARY

color names   shade   whistle

PREPARATION

- In advance, send a letter home asking that the children come in on a certain day wearing bright single-color shirts, or shirts of two or more colors if they have them. If this is not possible, use colorful sashes or arm bands.

WHAT TO DO

1. Ask the children to run around the playground until they hear the whistle, when they must stop, stand still, and listen.
2. When you say, "Spot that [color name] shirt!" they must all line up behind whoever has a shirt of that color.
3. Explain that if they are wearing a shirt of that color they must keep still and quiet and not shout out to the others to join them.
4. Remind them that there are many shades of each color, so that there may be four or five different people they could line up behind.
5. If there are only a few children, use several different colors each time. This will also help exercise their memories.
6. When you blow the whistle the children can all run around again, until you whistle again and call out another color.

TEACHER-TO-TEACHER TIP

- This is a good activity to do before a quiet activity because the children use a lot of energy.

ASSESSMENT

To assess the children's learning, consider the following:
- Talk about shirts in different shades of the color you called out.
- Did the children remember and follow instructions?

Children's Books

Aloha Shirt Colors by Kelly Sueda
In My New Yellow Shirt by Eileen Spinelli

Anne Adeney, Plymouth, England, United Kingdom

Traffic Lights

4+

LEARNING OBJECTIVES

The children will:
1. Become familiar with the colors green, yellow, and red.
2. Understand what traffic lights mean.

Materials

colored poster board
(red, green, yellow)
markers
pencils or craft sticks
sidewalk chalk
tape
plastic plates

VOCABULARY

footpath   road   safety   traffic rule
pedestrian

PREPARATION

● Cut a large circle from each of the three colors of poster board. Tape a pencil or craft stick on the back of each to serve as a handle.
● Draw crossroads on the sidewalk with chalk.

WHAT TO DO

1. Discuss the concept of the traffic lights with the children (red means stop, yellow means slow, green means go).
2. Let a child pretend to be a traffic controller and stand at the center of the crossroads to display the traffic lights one by one.
3. The other children can pretend to be cars and follow the traffic signs. Let the children use plastic plates as a steering wheel. A few children can act as pedestrians and walk across the marked crossing when the traffic light is red.
4. Children can interchange their roles and continue the game.

ASSESSMENT

To assess the children's learning, consider the following:
● Can the children identify the colors of each traffic light?
● Can the children explain the meaning of each color on a traffic light?

Shyamala Shanmugasundaram, Nerul, Navi Mumbai, India

Children's Books

Cars and Trucks and Things That Go by Richard Scarry
My Car by Byron Barton

Color Walk

3+

LEARNING OBJECTIVES

The children will:
1. Learn color recognition.
2. Explore the presence of color in nature.

Materials

clipboard
paper and pen

VOCABULARY

color names	match	rainbow	same

different

WHAT TO DO

1. Tell the children that colors are all around them in the classroom, in their homes, and in nature.
2. Take the children outdoors for a walk.
3. Call out a color, and ask them if they see anything that is that color.
4. On a clipboard, copy down the names of all the colored objects the children see.
5. Allow the children to name several objects for each color. Then, call out the next color.
6. Continue in this manner until the children find objects for all of the colors of the rainbow.
7. Once you are back in the classroom, ask the children to recall the colored objects that they saw on their walk. Check the list of objects you wrote on the clipboard to see how well the children can recall what they saw.

Children's Books

Brown Bear, Brown Bear, What Do You See? by Bill Martin, Jr.
Butterfly Butterfly: A Book of Colors by Petr Horacek
Colors Everywhere by Sam McBratney
Mouse Paint by Ellen Stoll Walsh
Planting a Rainbow by Lois Ehlert

ASSESSMENT

To assess the children's learning, consider the following:
• Can the children name foods whose colors match each of the colors in a rainbow?

Erin Huffstetler, Maryville, TN

Food for Thought

3+

LEARNING OBJECTIVES

The children will:

1. Develop oral language skills.
2. Identify colors.
3. Explore with five senses.

Materials

variety of colorful fresh
  fruits and vegetables
balance scale
tub

VOCABULARY

eat	smell	touch
fruits	taste	vegetables

WHAT TO DO

1. Display the fruits and vegetables in the science center along with a balance scale and tub full of water.
2. Help the children identify each fruit or vegetable and its color.
3. Invite the children to explore the fruits and other materials, weighing the items on the balance scale and testing whether a fruit or vegetable sinks or floats.
4. Suggest that the children compare sizes and textures of the various foods.
5. Afterwards invite the children to taste several of the food items as they talk about the color and the taste.

ASSESSMENT

To assess the children's learning, consider the following:

● Set one piece of fruit on a table. Ask one child to name the fruit and identify its color. Repeat with the remaining fruit and vegetables.

● Invite the children to sort the fruits and vegetables into groups according to color, size, or taste. Encourage the children to talk about their observations.

● Have the children sit in a single-file line, facing a tub of water. Pass one piece of fruit down the line. Ask the children to identify the fruits color and say its name. Once the fruit reaches the end of the line, have the last person set the fruit in a tub of water to find out if it sinks or floats. Repeat with different fruits or vegetables.

Mary J. Murray, Mazomanie, WI

Children's Books

Growing Vegetable Soup by Lois Ehlert
Is It Red? Is It Yellow? Is It Blue? by Tana Hoban

Hand Mixing

3+

LEARNING OBJECTIVES
The children will:
1. Discover that blending two or more colors makes a different color.
2. Experiment with paint.
3. Explore the feeling of mixing with their hands.

Materials

paper
tempera paint
shallow pans or dishes

VOCABULARY

blend	experiment	primary color	secondary color
combine	mix	print	

PREPARATION
● Pour red, yellow, and blue paint (primary colors) into shallow pans or dishes.

WHAT TO DO
1. Encourage the children to put one hand into a dish of primary colored paint and the other hand into another dish. Ask the children what color they think the two colors will make.
2. Then the children can rub their hands together to discover the new secondary color that resulted. Allow the children to press their hands onto paper to make prints.
3. Use one sheet of paper for each child or put all of the children's handprints on a large mural.
4. After the children wipe off their hands, they may wish to dip their hands into primary paints again and rub another child's hand to make a new color.

TEACHER-TO-TEACHER TIP
● Substitute magenta for red and turquoise for blue. Experiment to see how your paints blend best.

ASSESSMENT
To assess the children's learning, consider the following:
● Talk with the children about how blending colors makes different colors. Ask them to describe how the colors mix. It is not important that the children memorize what colors they form when they mix two colors, just that it is fun to experiment and discover on their own.

Children's Books

Little Blue and Little Yellow by Leo Lionni
Mouse Paint by Ellen Stoll Walsh

Laura Durbrow, Lake Oswego, OR

A Rainbow of Water Colors 3+

LEARNING OBJECTIVES

The children will:

1. Identify a rainbow of colors.
2. Learn what happens when you mix colors together.
3. Use small motor skills to create new colors.

Materials

water
food coloring
plastic containers (pill
   boxes with sections
   or plastic egg
   cartons)
eyedroppers (straws
   could be substituted)

VOCABULARY

blend   primary color   secondary color

WHAT TO DO

1. Give the children individual containers with water in them.
2. Allow the children to add a few drops of red, blue, and yellow food coloring to separate sections of the containers.
3. Provide eyedroppers or straws and encourage the children to take drops from one container and place them in an empty one.
4. Have the children add drops from one section to another and watch what happens. Help them identify the new colored water.
5. Use many containers to create new colors from the existing ones.

TEACHER-TO-TEACHER TIP

● To extend the activity, try painting on paper with the colors created, making a chart with all of the colors created, or creating sealed water bottles of each color for the science center.

ASSESSMENT

To assess the children's learning, consider the following:

● Review all the colors the children created with the food coloring and water.
● Are the children developing their small motor skills by using the eyedroppers and straws?

Children's Books

Color Dance by
Ann Jonas
Color Surprises by
Chuck Murphy
Mouse Paint by
Ellen Stoll Walsh

Michelle Barnea, Millburn, NJ

Be a Chameleon

4+

LEARNING OBJECTIVES

The children will:

1. Learn how chameleons adapt to their surroundings.
2. Demonstrate color awareness.

Materials

pictures of chameleons
construction paper
picture of a chameleon

VOCABULARY

camouflage   chameleon   protective   reptile

PREPARATION

● Show children the picture of a chameleon. Ask if anyone knows what it is (responses may include "gecko" or "lizard"). Ask how these types of creature move and what they eat.

WHAT TO DO

1. Tell the children about chameleons' unique color-changing qualities. Ask why it is good that the chameleon can do this (obtain food, hide, escape enemies).
2. Hold up the colors you plan to discuss (for example, red, green, and yellow). Name each color and ask children to repeat the name. Ask older children to name the colors without assistance, if possible.
3. Tell the children they are going to pretend to be chameleons, but they will change into the colors they are learning today.
4. Give each child one colored paper for each of the chosen colors. Tell the children they will hide like chameleons. When they hear the color and item that is "coming," they are to hold the correct color card in front of them.
5. Say, "Here comes a yellow dog!" The children should hold their yellow cards in front of them.
6. Ask the children to volunteer their own color statements for children to camouflage themselves.

ASSESSMENT

To assess the children's learning, consider the following:

● Call on a child to hold up a color. Can the other children call out the color's name?

Children's Books

Fake Out! Animals That Play Tricks by Ginjer L. Clarke
Leon the Chameleon by Melanie Watt
Rex by Ursula Dubosarsky

Terry Callahan, Easton, MD

Color-Coordinated Cuisines 4+

LEARNING OBJECTIVES

The children will:

1. Identify the colors in fruits and vegetables.
2. Learn about nutritious foods.

Materials

construction paper
child-safe scissors
magazines with
pictures of food (or
clip art)
glue sticks

VOCABULARY

health   mineral   nutrition   vitamin

PREPARATION

- Give each child a set of construction paper (with red, orange, brown, green, purple, yellow, and white).
- Set out child-safe scissors, magazines (or clip art), and glue sticks. If desired, cut out pictures of food in advance.

WHAT TO DO

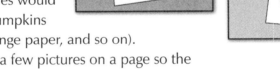

1. Ask the children to cut out pictures of food from magazines and sort them into piles by color.
2. Ask the children to glue foods on their matching color page (strawberries and cherries would go on the red paper, pumpkins and oranges on the orange paper, and so on). Demonstrate by gluing a few pictures on a page so the children get the idea.
3. As a class (or in groups) have the children share their food pages.
4. Discuss the importance of eating a variety of foods in each color. Explain the nutritional benefits these foods can provide.

TEACHER-TO-TEACHER TIP

- You can find a lot of information about the nutritional values of the fruits and vegetables listed above by visiting www.fruitsandveggiesmorematters.org and www.nlm.nih.gov.

ASSESSMENT

To assess the children's learning, consider the following:

- At the end of the activity, have the children share a page of their findings, either with the class or in groups.

Children's Books

Food for Healthy Teeth by Helen Frost
The Green Eaters: A Dream Come True by Jennifer Murphy
Prudence's Book of Food by Alona Frankel

Angela Hawkins, Denver, CO

Eye Color (Graph)

4+

LEARNING OBJECTIVES

The children will:

1. Compare their eye color to that of other children.
2. Observe differences and similarities.
3. Learn the names of various children's eye colors.

Materials

pocket chart (optional)
name cards for each
   child in the group
tagboard
pictures of three or
   four colors of eyes

VOCABULARY

blue	eyes	less
brown	hazel	more

PREPARATION

- Make a header card using tagboard with the question "What Color Are Your Eyes?"
- Place pictures of eyes to represent different columns. Label the colors under the pictures (blue, hazel, brown).

WHAT TO DO

1. Place the header card in the top row of a pocket chart.
2. Ask the children to place their names in the appropriate column in the pocket chart to indicate their eye color.
3. Discuss the results. Are there more blue eyes or brown?
4. Challenge the children to group themselves based on eye color.
5. Once the children group themselves by eye color, ask them to line up, forming a human graph.

What color are your eyes?

blue	hazel	brown
	Carl	
	Allie	
Andy	Emile	Kate
Lisa	Jansen	Tai
👀 blue	👀 hazel	👀 brown

TEACHER-TO-TEACHER TIP

- Laminate the header card and name cards for durability.

ASSESSMENT

To assess the children's learning, consider the following:

- Can the children identify their own eye color?
- Can they identify children in the class who have the same eye color?

Children's Books

Arthur's Eyes by
   Marc Brown
Colors! ¡Colores! by
   Jorge Lujan
Of Colors and Things
   by Tana Hoban
*White Rabbit's Color
Book* by Alan Baker

Jackie Wright, Enid, OK

Ladybugs Are Black and Red

4+

Materials

books and magazines
    with pictures of
    ladybugs
drawing paper
crayons

LEARNING OBJECTIVES

The children will:
1. Learn to identify ladybugs.
2. Learn why ladybugs are beneficial.

VOCABULARY

beneficial   garden   helpful   insect
bug

PREPARATION

- Place paper and crayons on the tables. On each table, have ladybug pictures for the children to look at and copy if they want.

WHAT TO DO

1. Sit in a circle and talk about ladybugs. Ask the children if they have seen ladybugs or know anything about them. Do the children know that ladybugs are helpful insects because they eat bugs that eat plants?
2. Encourage the children to talk about plants and bugs, flowers and gardens, and how these are interrelated.
3. Show them pictures of ladybugs in books or magazines. Also show pictures of other insects so they can see the differences.
4. The children will draw and color ladybug pictures at the tables. Have them write their names on the pictures. Display their artwork. Encourage family members and caregivers to look at their children's pictures.

POEM

I Love Ladybugs by Shirley Anne Ramaley
I love ladybugs,   *They eat lots of bugs*
Do you know?   *So plants will grow!*

ASSESSMENT

To assess the children's learning, consider the following:
- Ask the children, "What colors are ladybugs?"
- Show the children pictures of ladybugs and other insects. Can they find the ladybugs?
- Can the children explain why farmers and gardeners like ladybugs?

Children's Books

Are You a Ladybug? by
    Judy Allen
The Grouchy Ladybug
    by Eric Carle
A Ladybug's Life by
    John Himmelman
Ten Little Ladybugs by
    Melanie Gerth

Shirley Anne Ramaley, Sun City, AZ

What Is Blue?

4+

LEARNING OBJECTIVES

The children will:

1. Identify the color blue.
2. Distinguishing shades of blue.
3. Organize and group according to shades of blue.

Materials

roll of paper
variety of blue coloring
media

VOCABULARY

cobalt blue	light blue	pale	sapphire
dark blue	navy blue	powder blue	sky blue

PREPARATION

- Roll a long piece of poster paper onto a table (or several tables set up end to end).
- Gather crayons, pastels, pencil crayons, and markers in many shades of blue.

WHAT TO DO

1. Ask the children to find all the blue toys and objects in the classroom and bring them to the table.
2. Help the children find a light blue and a dark blue toy or object. Put the lightest toy at one end of the table and the darkest at the other end.
3. Now help them arrange the other toys or objects between the lightest and darkest ends of the blue scale. You now have a blue scale on the table.
4. Next, help the children match the blue crayons, pastels, pencils, and markers to the blue objects on the table. These art media should make a similar graded blue scale.
5. The children can then use the shades of blue to color on the white paper, with lightest blue at one end of the paper and darkest blue at the other end.

TEACHER-TO-TEACHER TIP

- Allow children to color their own blue scales on a smaller paper.

ASSESSMENT

To assess the children's learning, consider the following:

- Engage the children in a discussion about the variety of hues that all fall into the category of "blue." Review how they created a blue scale to visualize their understanding.

Children's Books

Big Blue by Shelly Gill
I Love You, Blue Kangaroo! by Emma Chichester Clark

Patrick Mitchell, Yagoto, Nagoya, Japan

Flowers Are Many Colors

LEARNING OBJECTIVES

The children will:

1. Talk about the many colors of flowers.
2. Learn that colors attract bees and hummingbirds and other small creatures that pollinate the flowers.
3. Understand the meaning and importance of pollination.

Materials

crayons
coloring pages with
  flowers
poster board
magazines and books
  with pictures of
  flowers

VOCABULARY

fragrance	petal	pollinate	stem
leaf	pollen	seeds	

PREPARATION

● Place crayons, drawings of flowers to color, magazines and books with flower pictures, and plain poster board on tables for the children.

WHAT TO DO

1. Sit in a circle on the floor.
2. Ask the children, "What colors are flowers?" "Have you seen bees or hummingbirds or butterflies on flowers?"
3. Talk about the importance of colors in attracting these small creatures to flowers, and how colors help with pollination.
4. Explain that "pollination" means to transfer, or move, pollen from one flower to another and that it helps flowers make seeds so that new flowers will grow.
5. Have the children choose to draw flowers or put bees, hummingbirds, or butterflies on the flowers.
6. Ask the children to write their names on the papers. Display their artwork.

POEM

Roses Are Red (Traditional)

Roses are red,   Sugar is sweet,
Violets are blue.   And so are you!

ASSESSMENT

To assess the children's learning, consider the following:

● Show the children pictures of flowers. Can they name the colors and explain why colors are important to flowers?
● Are the children able to describe why bees are important to flowers?

Shirley Anne Ramaley, Sun City, AZ

Children's Books

Emily Is a Flower Girl by
  Claire Masurel
Flower Garden by
  Eve Bunting
*The Life Cycle of a
Flower* by Molly Aloian
One Hundred Flowers
  by Harold Feinstein
The Reason for a Flower
  by Ruth Heller

Sorting Buttons

3+

LEARNING OBJECTIVES

The children will:
1. Sort buttons by color.
2. Learn color names.
3. Develop small motor skills.

Materials

bowl or small tray for
  buttons
muffin tin
at least three buttons
  of each color
  (Choose large
  buttons [1"
  diameter] for three-
  year-olds. Smaller
  buttons may be used
  for older children.)

VOCABULARY

black	match	red	yellow
blue	orange	sort	
green	purple	white	

WHAT TO DO

1. Demonstrate how to sort the buttons.
2. One at a time, touch each button and say its color.
3. Touch two buttons of matching colors and place one button in a cup while repeating the color name.
4. Ask one child to find other buttons that are the same color.
5. Choose another color and work with the first child or another child until all the buttons are sorted.
6. Encourage the children to sort the buttons independently.

TEACHER-TO-TEACHER TIP

- Begin with primary colors. Then challenge the children by replacing colors with other colors such as pink and brown.

ASSESSMENT

To assess the children's learning, consider the following:
- Can the children describe how they sorted the buttons?
- In manipulating the buttons, are the children exhibiting age-appropriate small motor development?

Mary Jo Shannon, Roanoke, VA

Children's Books

Butterfly Butterfly: A Book of Colors by Petr Horacek
Colors by Anne Geddes

Not-So-Hungry Caterpillar 5+

LEARNING OBJECTIVES

The children will:

1. Develop an awareness of healthy diet, and identify healthy foods.
2. Demonstrate small motor skills by using a pencil or marker, safety scissors, and a glue stick.

Materials

magazines
child-safe scissors
lightweight cardboard
    such as from a
    cereal box or file
    folder
paper
markers

VOCABULARY

diet   healthy   nutritious

PREPARATION

● Cut the lightweight cardboard into enough 2" circles to give one to each child. These will be their circle patterns.
● Tear pictures of healthy foods out of the magazines.

WHAT TO DO

1. Discuss the importance of a healthy diet. Explain that eating healthy foods means eating very little junk food such as sweets and fast food. It also means not eating too much. Ask children, "What are healthy foods to snack on?" Explain that nutritious, healthy foods give us nutrients, vitamins, and other things we need to stay healthy.
2. Give each child a circle pattern and the pictures of healthy foods that you pulled out of the magazines.
3. Have the children look through the pictures for things they like to eat.
4. When they find a picture, they should trace their circle pattern on it and cut it out. They will each need five circles showing five different healthy foods.
5. Circulate among the children, helping them cut out the foods, arrange the circles in a row on a sheet of paper, and glue the circles down.
6. The children can use markers to draw eyes, antennae, and legs to complete a Not-So-Hungry Caterpillar.

ASSESSMENT

To assess the children's learning, consider the following:

● Are the children able to describe the foods in their circles and name the colors of their foods? Can they talk about why those foods are healthy?

Children's Books

I Will Never Not Ever Eat a Tomato by Lauren Child
Mmm, Cookies! by Robert Munsch

Sue Bradford Edwards, Florissant, MO

Colorful Snack: An End-of-Topic Celebration

3+

LEARNING OBJECTIVES

The children will:
1. Identify the color of foods.
2. Match food colors to spots on a placemat.
3. Use appropriate manners.
4. Taste a variety of foods.

Materials

white paper
colored construction
  paper circles
glue
contact paper
invitations
food in the colors you
  have taught
napkins
plastic plates and
  tableware

VOCABULARY

color names   menu items   please   thank you

PREPARATION

● Make placemats for each child by gluing colorful circles to white paper and covering them with contact paper.
● In advance, send out invitations to families and caregivers. Buy or ask families to supply foods in a variety of colors. Be aware of allergies when planning the menu. Make sure you have enough for all of the children to have at least one piece of each food.
● Set the table. Set up chairs for your guests.

WHAT TO DO

1. Welcome your guests and invite them to sit behind their children at the table.
2. Hold up each food item. Ask the children to identify it and its color. Have the children point to the colored spot on the placemat that matches what you hold up. Tell everyone that today's snack is a matching game. The children will show the family members where each food belongs on the placemat.
3. Remind them to say "please" and "thank you" and to practice other good manners.
4. As they eat, encourage the children to try unfamiliar foods.

ASSESSMENT

To assess the children's learning, consider the following:
● Are the children able to identify the color of each of the foods on their placemats?

Children's Books

Brown Bear, Brown Bear, What Do You See?
by Bill Martin, Jr.
Color Farm by
Lois Ehlert
Color Zoo by
Lois Ehlert

Debbie Vilardi, Commack, NY

Cream Cheese Colors

3+

LEARNING OBJECTIVES

The children will:
1. Recognize the change from one color to another.
2. Develop small motor skills.
3. Describe the taste of different foods.

Materials

whipped cream cheese
frozen strawberries or
   frozen blueberries,
   partially thawed
apple juice or water
blender (adult only)
small bowl per child at
   center
plastic spoons and
   knives
bagels, crackers, bread
napkins

VOCABULARY

blender	cream cheese	red/pink or blue/purple
change	puree	(depending on fruit used)

PREPARATION

- Set up food and blender in cooking center. Put bags of frozen fruit into bowls because they may leak as they thaw.

WHAT TO DO

1. Give each child a bowl with a large spoonful of cream cheese. Discuss the color of the cream cheese. Ask the children to sample a bit of the cheese and to describe the taste.
2. Have the children help put a half cup of berries into blender with two tablespoons of water or juice. Blend fruit (adult only) until it makes a puree (adjust the amount of liquid as needed). Discuss the color of the puree. Ask the children if the color changed in the blender.
3. Help the children pour a bit of puree into their cream cheese. Have the children stir the puree into the cream cheese. Ask the children to describe what is happening with the color of their cream cheese. Have them taste the cheese and discuss what it tastes like with the fruit puree.
4. Experiment with more and less puree to see the darker and lighter colors.
5. Serve with bagels, crackers, or bread for snack. Let the children spread the mixture themselves.

ASSESSMENT

To assess the children's learning, consider the following:
- Ask the children to describe what happened when they added the puree to the white cream cheese.

Cassandra Reigel Whetstone, Folsom, CA

Children's Books

Color Dance by Ann Jonas
The Color Kittens by Margaret Wise Brown
Red with Other Colors by Victoria Parker

Green Fruit Salad

3+

LEARNING OBJECTIVES

The children will:
1. Identify the color green.
2. Taste green fruits.

Materials

large bowl
honeydew melon
kiwis
green apples
green pears
green grapes

VOCABULARY

apples	green	kiwis	pears
grapes	honeydew melon		

PREPARATION

● Cut up the honeydew melon, kiwis, apples, and pears. Mix all the fruit in the bowl to create a big fruit salad.

WHAT TO DO

1. Offer the green fruit salad to the children. Have the children name the colors they see.
2. Ask the children to identify the fruits they see in the fruit salad. Name the fruits they do not recognize.
3. Encourage the children to describe the taste of the different fruits.

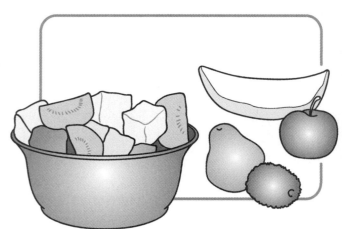

TEACHER-TO-TEACHER TIP

● Use green bowls, forks, and napkins to complement the green fruits.

ASSESSMENT

To assess the children's learning, consider the following:
● Review the colors of the foods the children ate. Can the children name the different fruits and then think of other foods that are green?

Laura Wynkoop, San Dimas, CA

Children's Books

Green by Sharon Gordon
Green Eggs and Ham by Dr. Seuss
Yummy Colors: A Pull-and-Pop Book by Beth Bryan

Fruit Rainbow

4+

LEARNING OBJECTIVES

The children will:
1. Sort fruits by colors.
2. Practice small motor skills.
3. Learn colors of the rainbow.
4. Learn about different fruits.

Materials

fruit (various colors;
   enough for entire
   group)
large preferably
   nonslip board
plastic knives
string

VOCABULARY

blueberry	cherry	pineapple	watermelon
cantaloupe	kiwi	sultana	

PREPARATION

- Prepare as much fruit as is needed for age of group.
- Mark out a rainbow on the nonslip surface, using the string.

WHAT TO DO

1. Tell the children that they are going to make a fruit rainbow for today's snack.
2. Ask the children to sort the fruit into colors and to name both the fruits and the colors.
3. If you are using any fruits that have different color skin and inside, identify these beforehand.
4. Engage the children in a discussion about blue, indigo, and violet colors and decide which fruits will fit best into this category, such as grapes, blueberries, or plums. Discuss the fact that it is difficult to find foods that fit well into the bright blue category.
5. Ask the children to wash their hands and then wash the fruit.
6. Encourage the children to help chop fruit using plastic knives.
7. Ask the children to arrange the fruit in curved rainbow layers, following the colors of the rainbow.
8. Remove the string and let the children serve the snack to the rest of the class.

Children's Books

The Magic School Bus Makes a Rainbow by Joanna Cole
Planting a Rainbow by Lois Ehlert
What Makes a Rainbow? by Betty Ann Schwartz

ASSESSMENT

To assess the children's learning, consider the following:
- Review the names of the fruits with the children.
- When they chop the fruit, challenge the children to cut pieces the same size as the rainbow bands on the boards.
- Can the children name the colors as they place the fruits on the correct band of the rainbow?

Anne Adeney, Plymouth, England, United Kingdom

Make a Shake

LEARNING OBJECTIVES

The children will:
1. Learn to follow a recipe.
2. Make a shake.
3. Design their shake on paper.

Materials

6 cups sliced
　　strawberries
2 cups ice
3 cups orange juice
small paper cups
blender (adult only)
straws (various colors)
basket
white construction
　　paper 8½" x 11"
child-safe scissors
crayons
felt pens
pastels
glue

VOCABULARY

blender	ice	shake	strawberries
colors	orange juice	straw	

PREPARATION

● Place strawberries, ice, and orange juice on the table with a blender.
● Place straws in a basket and place in the middle of the table.

WHAT TO DO

1. Demonstrate how to make the shake. Make half the recipe with one group and the other half of the recipe with the other group so all the children can participate. Give each child a turn placing the ingredients in the blender. Ask, "Can you put a few of the strawberries in the blender?" Pour in paper cups.
2. Give each child a piece of paper and crayons, felt pens, and pastels to draw their shake.
3. Ask the children to choose a straw to glue on the shake. Let dry.
4. Then ask them to print their names at the bottom of their shake.
5. At circle or group time, ask the children to point to their shakes. Say, "What color straw did you choose?" Encourage a discussion about color.

ASSESSMENT

To assess the children's learning, consider the following:
● Ask the children to describe their shakes.
● Ask the children how many straw colors there were, what types of colors they saw, and what ingredients they put in their shakes. Listen to each child's comments. Write down their comments if possible.

Lily Erlic, Victoria, British Columbia, Canada

Children's Books

Kids Cooking Without a Stove by Aileen Paul
Strawberries Are Red by Petr Horacek

Yummy Colors

LEARNING OBJECTIVES

The children will:

1. Learn colors using vegetables and fruits.
2. Identify healthy foods.
3. Learn two of the food groups.

Materials

broccoli (florets)
carrots (baby)
color cards
blueberries
strawberries
kiwi
eggplant
oranges
squash
tomatoes (grape)
sweet potatoes
plastic resealable bags
vegetable dip
colored paper plates

VOCABULARY

fruit	minerals	vegetable	vitamins
healthy	nutritious		

PREPARATION

- In advance, cut up the raw vegetables and fruits the children will eat.
- Keep one of each vegetable uncut so the children will know what it looks like in its natural state.
- Keep the food items in separate containers.

WHAT TO DO

1. Distribute six plates (one of each color) to every child.
2. Introduce the children to each fruit and vegetable, and its matching color card. Ask the children to say the name of the fruit or vegetable and the color of each.
3. Hold up each fruit and vegetable without the color card, and ask the children to identify the name and color of each fruit and vegetable.
4. Post the color cards on the board with tape.
5. If appropriate, challenge the children to use black washable markers to write the color names.
6. While the children work, fill the plastic bags with one piece of each fruit and vegetable, and distribute a bag to each child.
7. Ask the children to sort the fruits and vegetables according to color, and place them on the corresponding plates.
8. Invite the children to eat their samples.

ASSESSMENT

To assess the children's learning, consider the following:

- Review the colors of each plate by asking the children to read them aloud.
- Discuss with the children how they matched the color of each fruit and vegetable with the same colored plate.

Ann Francesco, Concord, NC

Children's Books

The Berenstain Bears and Too Much Junk Food by Stan and Jan Berenstain
The Green Eaters: A Dream Come True by Jennifer Murphy

Color, Color, Disappear! 3+

LEARNING OBJECTIVES

The children will:
1. Learn to name colors and match colors.
2. Learn and repeat a chant.

Materials

9" paper circles in red, orange, yellow, green, blue, and purple
colored chalk or dry-erase markers: red, orange, yellow, green, blue, and purple
eraser
chalkboard or dry-erase board

VOCABULARY

chant   disappear   reappear

PREPARATION

● Make circles on the board and color them in these colors: red, orange, yellow, green, blue, and purple.

WHAT TO DO

1. Place the 9" paper circles on the chalk or penholder below the colored circles drawn on the board.
2. Choose a child to erase one colored circle while the others chant the following rhyme, naming the color being erased:

Disappear, Circle by Susan Oldham Hill
Red circle, red circle, disappear! (child erases red circle)
Red circle, you are gone, I fear!
Now we see you reappear! (child holds up matching red circle)

3. Ask the child to hold up the matching circle as the children chant the last line. Repeat until all the circles are erased.

TEACHER-TO-TEACHER TIP

● To extend this activity, print with round cookie cutters in rainbow colors of paint.

ASSESSMENT

To assess the children's learning, consider the following:
● Can the children name the colors of the paper circles, and match them to a set of crayons?

Children's Books

The Art Lesson by Tomie dePaola
Little Blue and Little Yellow by Leo Lionni
Mouse Paint by Ellen Stoll Walsh
Of Colors and Things by Tana Hoban

Susan Oldham Hill, Lakeland, FL

Color-Match March

3+

LEARNING OBJECTIVES

The children will:
1. Learn to recognize colors.
2. Learn to match colors.

Materials

18" x 24" white
   construction paper
   in 3" widths, folded
   to make 1 ½" bands
crayons and markers
shape stickers in basic
   solid colors
stapler (adult only)
two sets of crayons

VOCABULARY

blue	orange	red
green	purple	yellow

WHAT TO DO

1. Ask the children to choose a single color and use materials of that color to make a headband. Help the children staple their headbands.
2. Ask the children to get into color groups by matching their headbands.
3. Explain the march: Each color group will chant the words for their color while marching with knees high.

   Color March by Susan Oldham Hill
   See the colors march so proud!
   Hear them say their names out loud!
   Red on an apple, and on a stop sign;
   Red tomatoes, all in a line.
   See the colors march so proud!
   Hear me say my name out loud: Red! Red! Red!

4. Repeat the rhyme, using the following two lines for the middle verses and repeating the name of the color three times at the end:

   Yellow on bananas, yellow in the sun;
   Yellow on canaries, yellow is fun!

   Blueberries, bluebirds flying high;
   Big blue ocean and big blue sky!

   Orange in an orange and in the morning sky;
   Orange in a carrot and sweet potato pie!

   Purple in a violet and eggplant, too;
   Purple in a plum and eggplant, it's true!

ASSESSMENT

To assess the children's learning, consider the following:
● Ask the children, one by one, to name the colors of one set of crayons. Can the children match the crayons from one set to those in the other set?

Children's Books

Color Dance by
   Ann Jonas
*Mr. Rabbit and the
   Lovely Present* by
Charlotte Zolotow
Red Is Best by
Kathy Stinson

Susan Oldham Hill, Lakeland, FL

Suzy Had a Bright Red Dress 3+

LEARNING OBJECTIVES

The children will:

1. Practice color and object recognition.
2. Follow directions.

Materials

paper cutouts for each child of a red dress, a blue car, a purple ball, and two yellow blocks

VOCABULARY

ball   car   color names   dress
blocks

PREPARATION

- Give each child a set of paper cutouts.
- Review what each cutout is with the children.

WHAT TO DO

Sing the following song while children hold up the corresponding paper cutouts. Optional motions for children are included.

Suzy Had a Bright Red Dress by Sarah Stasik

Suzy had a bright red dress, (children sway red paper dress back and forth)
Bright red dress, bright red dress.
Suzy had a bright red dress,
She wore it every day.

Jacob had a purple ball, (children pretend to "throw" purple paper ball softly)
Purple ball, purple ball.
Jacob had a purple ball,
He threw it every day.

Adam had a dark blue car, (children move blue paper car back and forth like they are rolling it)
Dark blue car, dark blue car.
Adam had a dark blue car,
He rolled it every day.

Lisa had some yellow blocks, (children pretend to stack paper blocks on top of each other in the air)
Yellow blocks, yellow blocks.
Lisa had some yellow blocks,
She stacked them every day.

Children's Books

Brown Bear, Brown Bear, What Do You See? by Bill Martin, Jr.
Mary Wore Her Red Dress and Henry Wore His Green Sneakers by Merle Peek

ASSESSMENT

To assess the children's learning, consider the following:

- To assess and enhance the children's color recognition skills, ask them to name the colors of their clothes, or the color of toys they like to play with. Can the children incorporate those colors into drawings?

Sarah Stasik, Roanoke, VA

Where Is Blue Bird?

3+

LEARNING OBJECTIVES

The children will:

1. Listen to and participate in a fingerplay or song about two birds.
2. Use color names as they relate to the poem.

Materials

jumbo craft sticks or dowels

tagboard or construction paper in up to eight basic colors

glue or tape

VOCABULARY

bird   echo   fly   poem

color names

PREPARATION

● Cut out two birds of each of the chosen color. Laminate the birds for durability.

● Glue or tape the birds to craft or dowel sticks to make a stick puppet. Make two pairs of puppets for each color. Separate the birds into two piles, one of each color for each hand.

WHAT TO DO

1. Hide the puppets behind your back.
2. Gather the children and tell them that you have new friends to introduce to them.
3. Hold the first two (the blue ones) in your hands and begin to sing the following song, using the birds to match the actions the song describes:

Where Is Blue Bird by Shelley Hoster
(Tune: "Where Is Thumbkin?")
Where is blue bird, where is blue bird?   *How are you today, sir?*
Here I am, Here I am.   *I think I'll fly away, sir.*
       Then, fly away, fly away!

4. Repeat the song with other colors until all the birds have been revealed. Then sing the last verse:

Where are all the birds, where are all   *We can name your colors now,*
*   the birds?*   *All of you have shown us how!*
Here we are, here we are!

ASSESSMENT

To assess the children's learning, consider the following:

● Can the children locate and name other classroom objects that are the same colors as the images of the birds?

● Can the children act out the fingerplay themselves for their friends?

Children's Books

Birds, Nests, and Eggs by Mel Boring
A Color of His Own by Leo Lionni
Color Dance by Ann Jonas

Shelley Hoster, Norcross, GA

Cats Come in Many Colors 4+

LEARNING OBJECTIVES

The children will:

1. Learn about the colors of cats.
2. Talk about cats they know, share their knowledge, and increase their self-esteem.
3. Learn that calico cats are orange, black, and white, and that tabby cats are usually striped but can be spotted or have other patterns.

Materials

drawing paper or
  poster board
crayons
pictures of various
  colored cats

VOCABULARY

calico   solid   tabby

WHAT TO DO

1. Sit in a circle with the children and ask them if anyone has cats at home. If they do not, their grandparents or friends may have cats.
2. Encourage the children to talk about the cats they know. Ask about the colors of cats. What colors have they seen? Do they know the meaning of "calico" and "tabby?"
3. Teach them the following fingerplay:

Five Tabby Kittens by Shirley Anne Ramaley
Five tabby kittens, sitting by my door. (hold up five fingers)
One fell asleep and then there were four. (hold up four fingers)
Four tabby kittens playing by a tree,
One chased a mouse, and then there were three. (hold up three fingers)
Three tabby kittens, wondering what to do.
One went to eat and then there were two. (hold up two fingers)
Two tabby kittens sleeping in the sun.
One woke up and ran. Then there was one. (hold up just one finger)
One tabby kitten, sitting all alone.
He quickly got up and ran right home.
And then there were none! (close hand, then clap)

ASSESSMENT

To assess the children's learning, consider the following:

● Show the children pictures of cats and ask them to name their colors. Discuss what *calico* and *tabby* mean. Ask the children to describe other colors that cats might be.

Children's Books

The Cat in the Hat by
  Dr. Seuss
Millions of Cats by
  Wanda Gag

Shirley Ann Ramaley, Sun City, AZ

Color Patterns Song

4+

LEARNING OBJECTIVES

The children will:
1. Learn to identify colors.
2. Build and recognize patterns.

Materials

three red blocks
three blue blocks
two yellow blocks
two green blocks

VOCABULARY

blue	red	yellow
pattern	repetition	

WHAT TO DO

1. Have each child make three stacks of blocks using the following color patterns (if there are not enough blocks, let children make stacks in small groups, or make one set of stacks for the entire group):
   - stack 1: red, blue, yellow
   - stack 2: red, blue, green
   - stack 3: red, blue, green, and yellow.
2. Sing the following song, encouraging the children to point to the correct stack of blocks for each verse.

   Red, Blue, Yellow by Sarah Stasik
   (Tune: "Are You Sleeping?")
   Red, blue, yellow,   Red, blue, green, and yellow,
   Red, blue, yellow.   Red, blue, green, and yellow.
   Red, blue, green,   Red, blue, green,
   Red, blue, green.   Red, blue, green.

ASSESSMENT

To assess the children's learning, consider the following:
- Ask younger children to dismantle the blocks and then recreate the stacks as they sing the song. This helps promote listening skills, as well as helps the children develop their visual memory.
- For older children, set out crayons and paper and challenge them to draw the stacks, putting the correct colors in the correct order.

Sarah Stasik, Roanoke, VA

Children's Books

Pattern by
Henry Arthur Pluckrose
Pattern Bugs by
Judy Harris

Five Little Crayons

4+

LEARNING OBJECTIVES

The children will:

1. Learn the names of colors.
2. Distinguish between colors.
3. Learn and repeat a rhyme.

Materials

a box of eight basic colors
colored squares or counters for each child

VOCABULARY

color names	lime	sunshine
grizzly bear	stop sign	

PREPARATION

● Make a chart with the words to the fingerplay below, using colored markers to match the color names used in the fingerplay.

WHAT TO DO

1. Teach the children the following fingerplay. Ask them to hold up the correct colored square or counter to match the color mentioned in the fingerplay.

   Five Little Crayons by Susan Oldham Hill
   Five little crayons ready to draw
   The most colorful picture you ever saw.
   The red one said, "I'll make a stop sign."
   The green one said, "I'll color a lime."
   The yellow one said, "I'll draw sunshine in the air."
   The brown one said, "I'll make a grizzly bear."
   The blue one said, "I'll color in the sky."
   So they used their colors to make things shine.
   Five little crayons ready to draw
   The most colorful picture you ever saw.

2. Mention other colors and items traditionally seen in that color, such as carrots for orange.
3. Ask the children to find the color names in the poem.
4. Ask them to look for two lines that are the same.

ASSESSMENT

To assess the children's learning, consider the following:

● Can the children repeat the song on their own?
● Can the children look in a box of crayons to identify the colors they name in the song?

Children's Books

The Art Lesson by Tomie dePaola
Color Dance by Ann Jonas
Is It Red? Is It Yellow? Is It Blue? by Tana Hoban
Look at Rainbow Colors by Rena K. Kirkpatrick

Susan Oldham Hill, Lakeland, FL

Color Me Gone

3+

LEARNING OBJECTIVES

The children will:
1. Practice listening and waiting skills.
2. Search for and recognize hues of colors.

Materials

A group of colorfully clothed children

VOCABULARY
dark   light   wearing

PREPARATION
● Notice the colors of the clothing that the children are wearing.

WHAT TO DO
1. Make a big show of looking around at everyone.
2. Notice the children who are doing what you asked (sitting quietly at circle, cleaning up) and comment on a certain article of clothing of a particular color they are wearing.
3. Let these children transition to the next classroom activity. For example, "I see Darla and Joey are wearing light green shirts. Anyone who is wearing a light green shirt may go to the snack table." "Anyone who has purple shoelaces may go to the snack table."
4. Continue until all children have been dismissed to the next activity. If the children are waiting in line, you can do this activity to help them wait. "Anyone who is wearing a dark blue belt, shake your hands in the air." "Anyone who has black shoes, hold out your arms like an airplane."

TEACHER-TO-TEACHER TIPS
● This is a fun activity to do as a transition from one activity to another, such as circle or group time to the snack table.
● Make this activity even more fun by designating two colors or two articles of clothing, such as a blue top and blue socks or a red top and white shoelaces. Introduce different patterns, such as stripes, polka dots, or plaid.

ASSESSMENT
To assess the children's learning, consider the following:
● Ask the children to listen carefully to the color names you call out and engage them in conversation about following directions. Are they able to identify the colors they are wearing?

Children's Books

The Emperor's New Clothes by Hans Christian Andersen
New Clothes for New Year's Day by Hyun-joo Bae

Kay Flowers, Summerfield, OH

Color Captain

4+

LEARNING OBJECTIVES

The children will:

1. Listen for and identify colors.
2. Improve their skills at following directions.

Materials

colorful curling ribbon
streamers
pencil or dowel
colorful hat

VOCABULARY

colors   hat   wait   wand

PREPARATION

● Create a colorful wand by taping several strands of colorful curling ribbon and crepe paper streamers to the end of an unsharpened pencil or wooden dowel.

WHAT TO DO

1. Add color to transition time with a colorful wand and hat.
2. Invite one child to wear the hat and hold the wand.
3. Designate a specific group of children who are ready to move on to the next activity: "The children who are wearing a red shirt may move on," and so on.
4. After you announce the specific color group, the "Color Captain" walks around the room and taps the children that fit into the group with the wand.
5. As each child is touched, she may line up or move on to the next activity.
6. Continue calling out color groups until the "Color Captain" taps each child with the wand and the entire class has moved on to the next activity.

TEACHER-TO-TEACHER TIP

● Each day, allow a different child to be the Color Captain.

ASSESSMENT

To assess the children's learning, consider the following:

● Invite each child to use the wand to point out other color items within the classroom. Wave the wand through the air as you name a color. Invite children to search the room to find a small object of that color and bring it to the circle area. Have each child tell about her object. Call out a new color and wave your wand again. Continue the activity until children have identified all the colors.

Children's Books

Art School by Mick Manning
Is It Larger? Is It Smaller? by Tana Hoban

Mary J. Murray, Mazomanie, WI

Index of Children's Books

A

The Adventures of Melon and Turnip by Trisha Adelena Howell, 65

Agrupemos Alimentos/Sorting Foods by Patricia Whitehaus, 65

All About Colors by Ruth Thomson, 46

Aloha Shirt Colors by Kelly Sueda, 80

Apples and Oranges: Going Bananas with Pairs by Sara Pinto, 48

Are You a Ladybug? by Judy Allen, 89

The Art Lesson by Tomie dePaola, 100, 106

Art School by Mick Manning, 108

Arthur's Eyes by Marc Brown, 88

B

Barrels to the Moon by Harold Berson, 56

Batty for Black by Christianne C. Jones, 55

The Berenstain Bears and Too Much Junk Food by Stan & Jan Berenstain, 99

Big Blue by Shelly Gill, 90

The Big Honey Hunt by Stan & Jan Berenstain, 24

Big Ones, Little Ones by Tana Hoban, 41

Birds, Nests, and Eggs by Mel Boring, 103

Blue Hat, Green Hat by Sandra Boynton, 18

Bread and Cereal by Tea Benduhn, 61

Brown at the Zoo by Christianne C. Jones, 55

Brown Bear, Brown Bear, What Do You See? by Bill Martin Jr., 23, 30–31, 36, 58, 66, 71, 82, 94, 102

Butterfly Butterfly: A Book of Colors by Petr Horacek, 35, 82, 92

Butterfly Express by Jane Belk Moncure, 45

C

Caps for Sale by Esphyr Slobodkina, 23

Cars and Trucks and Things That Go by Richard Scarry, 81

The Cat in the Hat by Dr. Seuss, 104

Cat's Colors by Jane Cabrera, 12, 34, 38

Chicka Chicka Boom Boom by Bill Martin Jr., 20

Chicka Chicka, 1, 2, 3 by Bill Martin Jr., 31, 1, 2, 3, 36

Chidi Only Likes Blue: An African Book of Colors by Ifeoma Onyefulu, 12

City Colors by Zoran Milich, 51–52

Color by Ella Dorran, 51

Color Dance by Ann Jonas, 10, 28, 74–75, 78, 85–86, 95, 101, 103, 106

Color Farm by Lois Ehlert, 28, 30, 57, 94
The Color Kittens by Margaret Wise Brown, 25, 95
A Color of His Own by Leo Lionni, 22, 46, 48, 56–58, 64, 103
Color Surprises by Chuck Murphy, 85
Color Zoo by Lois Ehlert, 30, 32, 44, 62, 66, 94
Colors and Shapes/Los colores y las figures by Gladys Rosa-Mendoza, 73
Colors by Anne Geddes, 92
Colors by Dorling Kindersley, 52
Colors Everywhere by Sam McBratney, 82
Colors Everywhere by Tana Hoban, 29, 32, 43, 78
The Colors of Us by Karen Katz, 17
Colors!/¡Colores! by Jorges Lujan, 88
Colors/Los Colores by Clare Beaton, 10
Colors: Green by Esther Sarfatti, 60

D
Dog's Colorful Day by Emma Dodd, 26–27

E
Eating Fractions by Bruce McMillan, 39
Ella Sarah Gets Dressed by Margaret Chodos-Irvine, 40
Elmer by David McKee, 26
Elmer's Colors by David McKee, 11
Emily Is a Flower Girl by Claire Masurel, 91
The Emperor's New Clothes by Hans Christian Andersen, 107

F
Fake Out! Animals That Play Tricks by Ginjer L. Clarke, 86
Fletcher and the Falling Leaves by Julia Rawlinson, 33
Flower Garden by Eve Bunting, 91
Food for Healthy Teeth by Helen Frost, 87
Food for Thought by Saxton Freymann, 39
Freight Train by Donald Crews, 69
From Caterpillar to Butterfly by Deborah Heiligman, 42

G
Giraffe Graphs by Melissa Stewart, 64, 68
Good Night, Sweet Butterflies by Dawn Bentley et al., 42
Graphs by Bonnie Bader, 68
Green as a Bean by Karla Kuskin, 60

Green by Sarah L. Schuette, 60

Green by Sharon Gordon, 96

The Green Eaters: A Dream Come True by Jennifer Murphy, 87, 99

Green Eggs and Ham by Dr. Seuss, 96

Green Wilma by Tedd Arnold, 53

The Grouchy Ladybug by Eric Carle, 89

Growing Vegetable Soup by Lois Ehlert, 83

H

Harold and the Purple Crayon by Crockett Johnson, 20, 53, 69

Hokey Pokey: Another Prickly Love Story by Lisa Wheeler, 70

Honey … Honey … Lion! by Jan Brett, 24

The Honey Makers by Gail Gibbons, 24

How Is a Crayon Made? by Oz Charles, 9

I

I Like Cereal by Jennifer Julius, 61

I Love Colors by Margaret Miller, 59, 70, 72

I Love Colors! by Hans Wilhelm, 38, 43

I Love You, Blue Kangaroo! by Emma Chichester Clark, 90

I Spy Colors in Art by Lucy Micklethwait, 51

I Will Never Not Ever Eat a Tomato by Lauren Child, 93

In My New Yellow Shirt by Eileen Spinelli, 80

Is It Larger? Is It Smaller? by Tana Hoban, 108

Is It Red? Is It Yellow? Is It Blue? by Tana Hoban, 29, 34, 54, 83, 106

K

Kid Tea by Elizabeth Ficocelli, 51

Kids Cooking Without a Stove by Aileen Paul, 98

L

A Ladybug's Life by John Himmelman, 89

Leon the Chameleon by Melanie Watt, 86

The Life Cycle of a Flower by Molly Aloian, 91

Little Blue and Little Yellow by Leo Lionni, 10, 22, 54, 84, 100

Living Color by Steve Jenkins, 32

Look at Rainbow Colors by Rena K. Kirkpatrick, 106

Looking at Paintings: An Introduction to Fine Art for Young People by Erika Langmuir, 14

M

Maddie Wants New Clothes by Louise Leblanc, 40

The Magic School Bus Makes a Rainbow by Joanna Cole, 97

Maisy's Color Collection by Lucy Cousins, 28

Marcos Colors: Red, Yellow, Blue by Tomie dePaola, 54

Mary Wore Her Red Dress and Henry Wore His Green Sneakers by Merle Peek, 21, 102

Midnight Snowman by Caroline Feller Bauer, 56

Millions of Cats by Wanda Gag, 104

The Mixed Up Chameleon by Eric Carle, 58

Mmm, Cookies! by Robert Munsch, 93

Mouse Paint by Ellen Stoll Walsh, 13, 19, 27, 29–31, 46, 50, 74–75, 82, 84, 100

Mouse's First Fall by Lauren Thompson, 33

Mr. Rabbit and the Lovely Present by Charlotte Zolotow, 101

My Car by Byron Barton, 81

My Colors by Rebecca Emberley, 77

My Crayons Talk by Patricia Hubbard, 19–20, 26, 59

My Hands Can by Jean Holzenthaler, 57

My Many Colored Days by Dr. Seuss, 51, 52, 62, 73

My Very First Book of Colors by Eric Carle, 62, 66, 71–72

N

Nature's Paintbrush: The Patterns and Colors Around You by Susan Stockdale, 77

New Clothes for New Year's Day by Huyn-joo Bae, 107

O

Of Colors and Things by Tana Hoban, 15, 34, 78, 88, 100

One Fish, Two Fish, Red Fish, Blue Fish by Dr. Seuss, 22–23, 31

One Hundred Flowers by Harold Feinstein, 91

One Saturday Morning by Barbara Baker, 56

¿Oso pardo, oso pardo, que ves ahi? by Bill Martin Jr., 71

P

A Pair of Socks by Stuart J. Murphy, 48, 50, 75

Pattern Bugs by Judy Harris, 105

Pattern by Henry Arthur Pluckrose, 105

Pink Takes a Bow by Christianne C. Jones, 55

Pinkalicious by Victoria & Elizabeth Kann, 21

Pip and Kip by Gina Erickson, 76

Planting a Rainbow by Lois Ehlert, 26, 30, 47, 49, 58, 65, 69, 82, 97

Polar Bear, Polar Bear, What Do You Hear? by Bill Martin Jr. & Eric Carle, 9, 36, 66

The Principal's New Clothes by Stephanie Calmenson, 21

Prudence's Book of Food by Alona Frankel, 87

Purple, Green, and Yellow by Robert Munsch, 17

R

Rain Drop Splash by Alvin Tresselt, 16

The Rainbow Fish by Marcus Pfister, 11, 16

A Rainbow of My Own by Don Freeman, 47

The Reason for a Flower by Ruth Heller, 91

Red by Karen Bryant-Mole, 72

Red Is a Dragon by Roseanne Thong, 71–72

Red Is Best by Kathy Stinson, 29, 101

A Red Train: A Colors Book by Bernette Ford, 35

Red with Other Colors by Victoria Parker, 13, 95

Red, Blue, Yellow Shoe by Tana Hoban, 10, 41, 43, 63, 79

Rex by Ursula Dubosarsky, 86

Ribbon Rescue by Robert Munsch, 63

S

Sam's Sandwich by David Pelham, 39

The Sandwich That Max Made by Marcia Vaughan, 39

Shapes by Jane Horne, 67

Shapes, Shapes, Shapes by Tana Hoban, 44, 67

Sort It Out by Barbara Mariconda, 61

Sorting by David Kirkby, 19, 41

Stone Soup by Marcia Brown, 49

Strawberries Are Red by Petr Horacek, 98

T

Teddy Bear Picnic by Jimmy Kennedy, 39

Ten Little Fish by Audrey Wood, 64

Ten Little Ladybugs by Melanie Gerth, 89

Three Little Kittens by Paul Galdone, 25

Tiger Math by Ann Whitehead Nagda, 68

V

The Very Hungry Caterpillar by Eric Carle, 42, 45

W

Warthogs Pain: A Messy Color Book by Pamela Duncan Edwards, 14
What Color Is It?¿Qué color es éste? by the editors of the American Heritage Dictionary, 18
What Color Is Your Underwear? by Sam Lloyd, 11
What Makes a Rainbow? by Betty Ann Schwartz, 15–16, 78, 97
When a Line Bends, a Shape Begins by Rhonda Gowler Greene, 67
White Rabbit's Color Book by Alan Baker, 10, 19, 27, 38, 43, 74, 88
Why Do Leaves Change Color? by Betsy Maestro, 33
Why Is the Sky Blue? by Chris Arvetis, 79
Winter White by Christianne C. Jones, 55

Y

Yellow Elephant: A Bright Bestiary by Julie Larios, 51
Yellow with Other Colors by Victoria Parker, 13
Yummy Colors: A Pull-and-Pop Book by Beth Bryan, 96

Z

Zak's Lunch by Margie Palatini, 39

Index

A

Accountability, 7
Adeney, Anne, 28, 40, 80, 97
Alike/different, 66, 88
Analytical thinking, 63
Apple juice, 95
Apples, 96
Arm bands, 80
Art activities, 8–18
Art materials, 99
Assessment, 7
Autumn, 33

B

Bagels, 95
Bags, 34, 41, 46, 61
    gift, 32
    resealable plastic, 10, 22, 99
Balance scales, 83
Bar graphs, 64, 68
Barnea, Michelle, 85
Baskets, 32–34, 43, 62, 98
    laundry, 50
    picnic, 39
Beach balls, 75
Beads, 28, 58
Beanbag pals, 69
Beanbags, 51
Bees, 24
Binders, 21
Bingo markers, 55
Bins, 77
Blankets, 39
Blenders, 95, 98
Blocks activities, 19
Blocks, 19, 105
Blueberries, 95, 99
Book activities, 20–26
Bowls, 14, 92, 95–96
    plastic, 19, 39, 96

Boxes, 23, 33, 40, 46, 77
    cereal, 93
    juice, 39
    pill, 85
    shoeboxes, 41
Bread, 95
Broccoli, 99
Bug catchers, 45
Bulletin board trim, 57
Bulletin boards, 38
Butcher paper, 20, 64
Butterflies, 42, 45
Buttons, 60, 92

C

Callahan, Terry, 86
Cameras, 21
Camouflage, 86
Candy wrappers, 11
Cantaloupes, 65
Caps, 23
Card stock, 11, 56, 59, 71
Cardboard, 93
Carrots, 99
Cash registers, 41
Cassette players, 52, 74, 76
Caterpillars, 42, 45
Cats, 104
CD players, 47, 52, 74, 76
Cereal, 61
Cereal boxes, 93
Chalk
    colored, 100
    sidewalk, 81
Chalkboards, 100
Chants, 30, 100
Chart paper, 25–26
Charting activities, 85, 106
Chenille stems, 45, 61
Choices, 18

Circle time activities, 27–37
Class books, 21, 26
Classifying, 12, 62
Clipboards, 82
Clothes, 50, 75, 80, 107
    doll, 40, 66
Clothespins, 35
Coffee cans, 62
Coffee mugs, 63
Collage materials, 9, 12
Collages, 12, 18
Color cards, 99
Color charts, 72
Color counters, 106
Color die, 29
Color flash cards, 37, 44, 49
Color scales, 90
Color words, 14–19, 21, 23, 26–30,
    32–33, 37, 41–43, 45–46, 49, 53,
    57, 59, 62, 67, 69–70, 78–79, 82,
    88, 100, 102–103
Colored balls, 77
Colored blocks, 19
Colored pencils, 55, 90, 99
Colored shape cards, 44
Colored squares, 106
Colored string, 64
Colored tape, 99
Coloring pages, 91
Comparing, 42, 63, 83, 88
Comprehension skills, 22
Construction paper, 15, 18, 27, 29–
    30, 37, 43, 47, 49, 54, 57, 59–60,
    62, 64, 71, 74, 78, 86–87, 94, 98,
    101, 103
Contact paper, 94
Cookie cutters, 100
Cooking activities, 94–99
Cooperation, 19, 37, 46, 50, 56, 77
Coordination, 70, 73

Cotton swabs, 17
Counting skills, 39, 42, 45, 60, 64
Crackers, 95
Craft jewels, 58
Craft sticks, 27, 81, 103
Crayons, 9, 20, 26, 29, 37, 54–55,
    67–68, 78, 89–91, 98, 101, 104–
    106
Cream cheese, 95
Creativity, 19
Crepe paper, 78–79
Cups, 61
    measuring, 98
    paper, 14, 98
    plastic, 19, 39
Curling ribbons, 108
Cutting boards, 97

D

Data collection, 68
Decision making, 28
Descriptors, 21
Die cuts, 35, 38, 62
Digital cameras, 21
Dishes, 84
Doll clothes, 40, 66
Dolls, 66
    paper, 66
    rag, 40
Dowel rods, 64, 103, 108
Dramatic play activities, 21, 23, 38–41
Dry-erase boards, 68, 100
Dry-erase markers, 68, 100
Durbrow, Laura, 84
Dzierzanowski, Holly, 22

E

Easels, 20, 25
Edwards, Sue Bradford, 68, 93
Egg cartons, 54, 85

Eggplants, 99
Eggs
    plastic, 77
Elastic bands, 99
Electrical tape, 13
Erasers, 100
Erlic, Lily, 98
Everham, Karyn F., 23, 53–54
Eyedroppers, 85
Eye-hand coordination, 51, 64, 75

F

Fabric, 11, 33, 53, 79
Fasteners, 40
Feathers, 99
Felt pens, 98
Felt, 10, 45
Fermino, Margery Kranyik, 18, 71, 73
File folders, 93
Fingerpaint paper, 10, 16
Fingerpaint, 10, 16
Fingerplays
    "Five Little Crayons" by Susan
      Oldham Hill, 106
    "Five Tabby Kittens" by Shirley
      Anne Ramaley, 104
    "Where Is Blue Bird?" by Shelley
      Hoster, 103
Flannel boards, 10
Flowers, Kay, 107
Following directions, 18, 35, 44, 50,
  52–53, 67, 71, 73, 79–80, 98, 102–
  108
Following rules, 77, 81
Food allergies, 24
Food coloring, 85
Food containers, 39
Food groups, 99
Forks, 96
Francesco, Ann, 99

Fruits, 83, 97
    apples, 96
    blueberries, 95, 99
    cantaloupes, 65
    grapes, 96
    honeydew melons, 65, 96
    kiwis, 96, 99
    oranges, 99
    pears, 96
    pictures, 87
    plastic, 39
    strawberries, 95, 98–99
    tomatoes, 99
    watermelons, 65
Funnels, 58

G

Game board spinners, 53
Games
    Butterfly Bonanza, 42
    Carton o' Primary Colors, 54
    Circle Color, 28
    Color Basket, 43
    Color Bingo, 55
    Color Card Game, 44
    Color Game, 51
    Color Search, 30
    Colorful Caterpillars, 45
    Find Your Favorite Color, 46
    I Can Sing a Rainbow, 47
    It's a Match, 48
    Make It a Whisper! 52
    Musical Colors, 74
    Rainbow Soup, 49
    Secondary Color Match-Up, 53
    Sock Walk, 50
    Swatch Match, 34
    What's My Color? 56
Gift bags, 32
Glitter, 9

Glue, 11, 15–16, 18, 44, 66, 76, 94, 98, 103
    sticks, 12, 55, 87, 93
Grape tomatoes, 99
Grapes, 96
Graphing activities, 64–65, 68
Grouping activities, 56, 90

H
Hammond, Janet, 36, 65, 77
Hats, 49, 108
Hawkins, Angela, 61, 87
Hill, Susan Oldham, 15–16, 29, 37, 78, 100–101, 106
Hole punches, 56
Honey, 24
Honeydew melons, 65, 96
Hoster, Shelley, 20, 26, 34, 103
Huffstetler, Erin, 48–49, 82
Hypotheses, 13

I
Ice, 98
Imagination, 13, 26
Index cards, 11
Invitations, 94

J
Juice boxes, 39
Juice
    apple, 95
    orange, 98

K
Kiwis, 96, 99
Knives, 96
    plastic, 95, 97

L
Lace ribbons, 76
Laminate, 38, 43–44, 47, 57, 88, 103

Language/literacy activities, 11, 12, 14, 17–20, 22, 24–26, 32, 39, 43–45, 56–59, 69–70, 83, 95, 98, 104
Large motor skills, 50–51, 73–77, 79–80
Laundry baskets, 50
Lawrence, Sherri, 67
Leaves, 9, 33
LeMasters, Carla, 43
Letter recognition, 27, 43
Letters home, 80
Lewandowski, Kaethe, 10
Library tape, 10
Life skills, 40
Listening skills, 35, 49, 55, 72, 74, 79, 105, 107, 108
Lucas, Eileen, 46, 66

M
Magazines, 12, 18, 38, 87, 89, 91, 93
Magnets, 64
Mallets, 72
Manners, 94
Markers, 9, 18, 52, 55, 57, 59–62, 64, 68, 71, 81, 90, 93, 101, 106
    dry-erase, 68, 100
    permanent, 58
    washable, 99
    white board, 59
Masking tape, 29, 35, 74–75
Matching activities, 16, 30, 32–34, 37–38, 40, 41, 44, 48–54, 57, 59, 64, 66, 77–78, 82, 87, 92, 94, 99–101
Math activities, 39, 42–43, 45, 60–68
Mayer, Carol, 25
Measuring cups, 98
Metamorphosis, 42
Miller, Jaclyn, 17, 70
Mitchell, Patrick, 9, 24, 59, 90

Mixing colors, 10, 13–14, 17, 22, 25, 27, 84–85, 95
Monochromatic painting, 14
Moran, Jane, 11
Morning greeting, 69
Muffin tins, 92
Mural paper, 42
Murals, 9, 84
Murray, Mary J., 19, 32, 39, 41–42, 44–45, 50, 52, 63, 69, 72, 75, 79, 83, 108
Music/movement activities, 70–76

N
Nagel, Sandra, 14, 21
Name cards, 88
Napkins, 39, 94–96
Newspaper, 25
Newsprint, 20
Note cards, 44
Number recognition, 43, 60, 64, 67
Nutrition, 65, 83, 87, 93–94, 96, 99

O
Orange juice, 98
Oranges, 99
Organizing data, 68
Outdoor activities, 56, 77–82

P
Page protector sleeves, 21
Pails, 77
Paint shirts, 14
Paint swatches, 34
Paint, 9, 11–14, 17, 55, 100
    pastels, 9, 24, 90, 98
    tempera, 25, 84
Paintbrushes, 13–14, 17, 25
Pans, 84
Paper cups, 14, 98

Paper dolls, 66
Paper plates, 24, 42, 99
Paper towels, 69
Paper, 9, 11–14, 17, 24–26, 32, 44, 65–67, 70, 82, 84, 89, 90, 93–94, 100, 102, 104–105
    butcher, 20, 64
    card stock, 11, 56, 59, 71
    chart, 25–26
    construction, 15, 18, 27, 29–30, 37, 43, 47, 49, 54, 57, 59–60, 62, 64, 71, 74, 78, 86–87, 94, 98, 101, 103
    contact, 94
    crepe, 78–79
    fingerpaint, 10, 16
    mural, 42
    newspaper, 25
    newsprint, 20
    tissue, 42
Paperclips, 64
Paste, 18
Pastels, 9, 24, 90, 98
Patterns, 61, 104, 105
Patton, Donna Alice, 55
Pears, 96
Pebbles, 58
Pencils, 13, 16, 55, 76, 81, 93, 108
    colored, 55, 90, 99
Pens, 11, 45, 82
    felt, 98
Percussion instruments, 72
Permanent markers, 58
Photocopiers, 17
Photos, 21
Pianos, 72
Picnic baskets, 39
Pictorial clues, 40
Pictures
    butterflies, 42

cats, 104
chameleons, 86
colors, 55
everyday items, 25
eyes, 88
flowers, 91
food, 87
healthy foods, 93
ladybugs, 89
rainbows, 16
stained-glass windows, 15
Pill boxes, 85
Placemats, 94
Plastic bottles, 58, 85
Plastic bowls, 19, 39, 96
Plastic containers, 24, 85
Plastic cups, 19, 39
Plastic eggs, 77
Plastic forks, 96
Plastic fruits, 39
Plastic knives, 95, 97
Plastic plates, 19, 39, 81, 94
Plastic spoons, 10, 58, 95
Plastic tableware, 94
Plastic tubs, 42
Plates
    paper, 24, 42, 99
    plastic, 19, 39, 81, 94
Play money, 41
Playdough, 22
Pocket charts, 57, 88
Poems
    "Color Bands" by Susan Oldham
        Hill, 78
    "Color March" by Susan Oldham
        Hill, 101
    "Disappear Circle" by Susan Old-
        ham Hill, 100
    "Favorite Colors" by Eileen Lucas,
        46
    "Five Little Crayons" by Susan
        Oldham Hill, 106
    "Green" by Laura Wynkoop, 60
    "I Love Ladybugs" by Shirley
        Anne Ramaley, 89
    "My Friends" by Anne Adeney,
        28
    "A Rainbow of Colors" by Laura
        Wynkoop, 35
    "Roses Are Red," 91
Pollination, 91
Pompoms, 9, 12
Positional words, 19, 23, 31
Poster board, 9, 34, 52, 55, 61, 65,
    68, 71, 81, 91, 104
Pots, 49
Predicting, 10, 13
Primary colors, 10, 17, 25, 54, 57–58,
    84–85, 92
Printers, 21
Prisms, 13
Puppets, 44
    stick, 103

Q
Quarles, Quazonia, 38

R
Rag dolls, 40
Rain, 13
Ramaley, Shirley Anne, 89, 91, 104
Rathbun, Angela, 12
Recorded music, 14, 47, 52–53,
    74–76
    Songs of Our World by Raffi, 18
Reilly, Jennifer, 64
Relational words, 65
Resealable plastic bags, 10, 22, 99
Rhythm, 72, 75–76
Ribbons, 9, 32, 53, 63

curling, 108
    lace, 76
Rivlin-Gutman, Annette, 13, 47
Romig, Hilary, 27
Rulers, 41, 55

S
Safety pins, 35
Sashes, 80
Science/nature activities, 10, 13, 17,
    22, 24, 33, 42, 82–91
Scissors, 11, 15–16, 18, 29, 42, 47,
    57, 59, 63, 71, 87, 93, 98
Secondary colors, 53, 57–58, 84–85
Sequencing, 47, 61, 105
Sequins, 9, 58
Shades, 12, 14, 24, 80, 90, 95, 107
Shallow pans, 84
Shanmugasundaram, Shyamala, 31,
    76, 81
Shannon, Mary Jo, 92
Shapes, 15, 22, 30, 43–44, 67, 70, 73,
    76
Sheets, 33
Shirts, 80
Shoeboxes, 41
Shoes, 41
Sidewalk chalk, 81
Signs, 41
Silk, 53
Sizes, 42, 63
Small motor activities, 9, 12, 15, 16,
    18, 40, 45, 57–58, 61, 85, 87, 95,
    92–98, 103
Smocks, 16
Snacks
    colorful, 94
    cream cheese colors, 95
    fruit rainbow, 97
    fruit shakes, 98

    fruits and vegetables, 83
    green fruit salad, 96
    melons, 65
    yummy colors, 99
Snaps, 40
Soap, 25
Social skills, 28, 36, 41, 46, 51, 56,
    58, 69, 77, 94
Socks, 50
Songs, 32
    "A Tisket, A Tasket," 43
    "Color Chain" by Susan Oldham
        Hill, 37
    "Color Song" by Margery Kranyik
        Fermino, 71
    "Colorful Caterpillar" by Mary J.
        Murray, 45
    "De Colores" by Raffi
    "The Green Grass Grows All
        Around" by Pete Seeger, 53
    "The Hokey Pokey," 70
    "I Can Sing a Rainbow," 47
    "I'm Bringing Home a Baby Bum-
        blebee," 24
    "It's Not Easy Being Green" by
        Jim Henson, 53
    "Mary Wore Her Red Dress," 21
    "Moving Colors" by Margery
        Kranyik Fermino, 73
    "Red, Blue, Yellow" by Sarah
        Stasik, 105
    "Red, Red Robin," 54
    "See Our Colors Fly" by Mary J.
        Murray, 79
    "Suzy Had a Bright Red Dress"
        by Sarah Stasik, 102
    "Where Is Blue Bird?" by Shelley
        Hoster, 103
    "Yellow Submarine," 54

Sorting activities, 11, 19, 23, 33, 38, 40, 45, 58, 61–62, 83, 92, 97, 99
Spelling, 59
Spoons, 14, 49
    plastic, 10, 58, 95
Squash, 99
Staplers, 29, 37, 78, 101
Stasik, Sarah, 56, 102, 105
Stick puppets, 103
Stickers, 9, 101
Sticks, 64
Sticky notes, 65
Storytelling activities, 20–22, 66
Strawberries, 95, 98–99
Straws, 85, 98
Streamers, 78–79, 108
String, 21, 97
    colored, 64
Stuffed animals, 39, 69
Sweet potatoes, 99

T
Tablecloths, 33
Tagboard, 16, 57, 88, 103
Taking turns, 19
Tape, 10–11, 47, 71, 81, 103
    colored, 99
    electrical, 13
    library, 10
    masking, 29, 35, 74–75
Teddy bears, 39
Tempera paint, 25, 84
Thread, 76
Timers, 46
Tints, 10, 12
Tissue paper, 42
Tissues, 16
Tomatoes, 98
Toy cars, 63
Traffic lights, 81

Transition activities, 107–108
Trays, 92
Trinkets, 58
T-shirts, 75
Tubs, 83

V
Vegetable dip, 99
Vegetables, 83
    broccoli, 99
    carrots, 99
    eggplants, 99
    grape tomatoes, 99
    pictures, 87
    squash, 99
    sweet potatoes, 99
Velcro, 34
Verbal cues, 55
Verdone, Jason, 62
Vilardi, Debbie, 30, 94
Visual memory, 105
Voting, 65

W
Waiting skills, 107
Washable markers, 99
Water, 13, 16, 24–25, 83, 85, 95
Watering cans, 13
Watermelons, 65
Websites, 87
Weighing, 83
Whetstone, Cassandra Reigel, 33, 95
Whistles, 56, 80
White board markers, 59
White boards, 59
Wright, Jackie, 57, 88
Writing activities, 11, 52, 59, 65
Wynkoop, Laura, 35, 60, 74, 96

X
Xylophones, 72

Y
Yarn, 56, 61, 99

Z
Zellerhoff, Freya, 51, 58
Zippers, 40

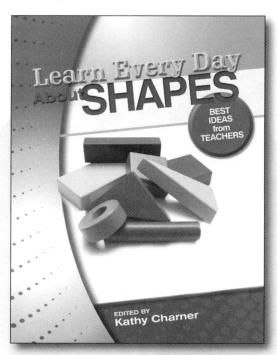

ISBN 978-0-87659-092-8
Gryphon House | 16247 | PB

ISBN 978-0-87659-090-4
Gryphon House | 15573 | PB

ISBN 978-0-87659-237-3
Gryphon House | 13963 | PB

ISBN 978-0-87659-238-0
Gryphon House | 14964 | PB

ISBN 978-0-87659-285-4
Gryphon House | 18595 | PB

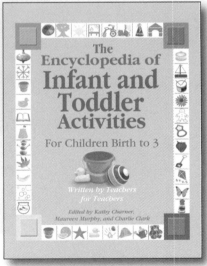

ISBN 978-0-87659-013-3
Gryphon House | 13614 | PB

the
GIANT
encyclopedia
of theme activities
for children
2 to 5

*Over 600 Favorite Activities
Created by Teachers
for Teachers*

ISBN 978-0-87659-166-6
Gryphon House | 19216 | PB

The
GIANT
Encyclopedia of
Math
Activities
For Children 3 to 6

*Written by Teachers
for Teachers*

*Edited by Kathy Charner,
Maureen Murphy, and Charlie Clark*

ISBN 978-0-87659-044-7
Gryphon House | 16948 | PB

The
GIANT
Encyclopedia of
Circle Time
and
Group Activities
for Children 3 to 6

*Over 600 Favorite Circle Time Activities
Created by Teachers for Teachers*

Edited by Kathy Charner

ISBN 978-0-87659-181-9
Gryphon House | 16413 | PB

The
GIANT
Encyclopedia of
Science
Activities
for Children 3 to 6

*More Than 600 Science Activities
Written by Teachers for Teachers*

Edited by Kathy Charner

ISBN 978-0-87659-193-2
Gryphon House | 18325 | PB

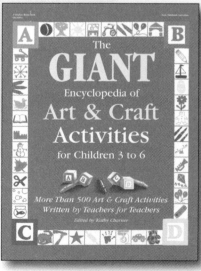

The
GIANT
Encyclopedia of
Art & Craft
Activities
for Children 3 to 6

*More Than 500 Art & Craft Activities
Written by Teachers for Teachers*

Edited by Kathy Charner

ISBN 978-0-87659-209-0
Gryphon House | 16854 | PB

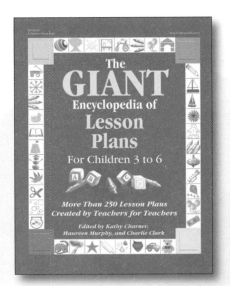

ISBN 978-0-87659-068-3
Gryphon House | 18345 | PB

ISBN 978-0-87659-012-6
Gryphon House | 15002 | PB

ISBN 978-0-87659-003-4
Gryphon House | 12635 | PB

ISBN 978-0-87659-001-0
Gryphon House | 11325 | PB